Oxford
Progressive
English Readers

FRANKE N ST

C000156598

The *Oxford Progressive English Readers* series provides a wide range of reading for learners of English.

Each book in the series has been written to follow the strict guidelines of a syllabus, wordlist and structure list. The texts are graded according to these guidelines; Grade 1 at a 1,400 word level, Grade 2 at a 2,100 word level, Grade 3 at a 3,100 word level, Grade 4 at a 3,700 word level and Grade 5 at a 5,000 word level.

The latest methods of text analysis, using specially designed software, ensure that readability is carefully controlled at every level. Any new words which are vital to the mood and style of the story are explained within the text, and reoccur throughout for maximum reinforcement. New language items are also clarified by attractive illustrations.

Each book has a short section containing carefully graded exercises and controlled activities, which test both global and specific understanding.

Frankenstein

Mary Shelley

Hong Kong
Oxford University Press
Oxford

Oxford University Press

Oxford   New York
Athens   Auckland   Bangkok   Bombay
Calcutta   Cape Town   Dar es Salaam   Delhi
Florence   Hong Kong   Istanbul   Karachi
Kuala Lumpur   Madras   Madrid   Melbourne
Mexico City   Nairobi   Paris   Singapore
Taipei   Tokyo   Toronto

and associated companies in
Berlin   Ibadan

Oxford is a trade mark of Oxford University Press

This adaptation first published 1993
This impression (lowest digit)
5   7   9   10   8   6   4

Illustrated by K.Y. Chan

Syllabus designer: David Foulds

Text processing and analysis by Luxfield Consultants Ltd

ISBN 0 19 585471 3

Printed in Hong Kong
Published by Oxford University Press (China) Ltd
18/F Warwick House East, Taikoo Place, 979 King's Road,
Quarry Bay, Hong Kong

CONTENTS

1 LETTERS FROM AN EXPLORER   1

2 THE EARLY LIFE OF VICTOR FRANKENSTEIN   12

3 THE MONSTER   22

4 THE TRIAL   34

5 THE RETURN OF THE DEMON   44

6 THE MONSTER'S EDUCATION   54

7 THE MONSTER'S REVENGE   65

8 FRANKENSTEIN TRAVELS TO ENGLAND   75

9 THE MARRIAGE   86

10 THE LONG CHASE   97

11 THE END OF THE EXPEDITION   107

   QUESTIONS AND ACTIVITIES   117

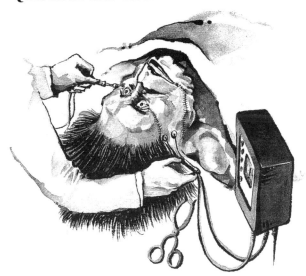

LETTERS FROM AN EXPLORER

Letter 1

From Robert Walton to his sister, Mrs Margaret Saville.

St. Petersburg, Russia, 11th December, 17__

My dearest Margaret,
    You will be very glad to know that I am safe, in spite of ⁵
*all your fears. I arrived yesterday and feel very confident
about the voyage of discovery that I plan to make.*
    *London seems a very long way off. Now, every day, when
I walk through the streets of St. Petersburg, a cold northern
wind blows upon my cheeks and fills me with delight. Do* ¹⁰
*you understand this feeling, my sweet sister? This wind has
come from the North Pole itself and it makes me dream of
that marvellous place, which I shall be the first to visit.*
    *It is no good people telling me that the Pole is covered
with frost or is just a freezing desert full of loneliness. I do* ¹⁵
*not believe it. In my imagination, the North Pole is a place
of beauty and delight. There, the sun never sets: it can
always be seen, just above the horizon, brightening
everything with a soft, gentle light. Earlier explorers thought
that snow and frost could not exist there. If they were right,* ²⁰
*we shall sail over a calm sea to a land which is more
beautiful and more wonderful than any place ever seen
before: a country of eternal light.*
    *Perhaps, when I am there, I shall be able to discover the
wonderful magnetic power which attracts the needles of* ²⁵
*compasses. I shall walk in places where no human being
has ever walked before. Thoughts of danger and death mean
nothing to me now. I feel the same joy and excitement that
a boy feels when he gets into a small boat with some friends
and sets out for the first time to explore the river he lives* ³⁰
beside.

But what if all these ideas are wrong? Even so, you cannot disagree, dear Margaret, that by sailing towards the North I shall be able to search for a passage from the Atlantic Ocean to the Pacific, or examine the secrets of the earth's
5 *magnetism. These things are certain to be of the greatest value to society.*

Ever since I was a child, this expedition has been a favourite dream of mine. I have read all the accounts of the various voyages which have been made in the hope of
10 *getting to the northern parts of the Pacific Ocean by sailing through the polar seas. You may remember that our good uncle Thomas's library consisted of nothing but books about all the voyages of discovery.*

I never went to school, or had a teacher, but you will
15 *remember that I loved reading and I studied those books day and night. I longed to go on similar voyages myself. I was very disappointed when I learned it was my father's dying wish that*
20 *my uncle should never allow me to go to sea.*

These ideas faded as I grew older. When I started to read literature, I became much more interested in that. You remember I also became a poet and imagined that I might become famous for my poetry. You know that I failed and that I was greatly disappointed. But just at that time, my cousin died and left me some money, and my thoughts turned back to my earlier interest.

Six years have passed since I first decided to prepare for this expedition. I began by strengthening my body in order to stand up to the hardships I knew I would have to face. I went whale hunting several times in the North Sea. I learned to conquer cold, hunger, thirst and lack of sleep. I worked harder than the ordinary sailors during the day, and spent all my nights studying mathematics, medicine and science so that I might be able to meet any danger or difficulty. Twice I worked as an officer in a whaling ship that sailed to Greenland. I felt very proud when the captain asked me to remain with him as his second in command.

Do you not think I deserve to achieve my aims, Margaret? If I wanted to, I could pass my life in ease and comfort, but I prefer glory to anything that money can buy. My courage is firm, but my hopes are forever changing, and my spirits are often depressed. I am about to start on a long and difficult voyage, and will need to be well prepared for every difficulty; I am required not only to raise the spirits of others, but sometimes to keep up my own, too.

I shall leave St Petersburg three weeks from now and travel north, by sledge, to Archangel. There I shall hire a boat and employ some men who are experienced whale hunters. I shall set sail in June when the weather will be at its best. And when shall I return? Ah, dear sister, how can I answer this question? If I succeed, many, many months, perhaps years, will pass before you and I may meet again. If I fail, you will see me soon — or never.

Farewell, my dear, excellent Margaret.
Your affectionate brother,

Robert Walton.

Letter 2

Archangel, Russia, 28th March, 17__

My dearest Margaret,

All around us here there is nothing but frost and snow,
5 *and the time passes very slowly, yet a second step has been*
taken towards my expedition. I have hired a ship, and am
now busy looking for sailors to come with me. Those whom
I have already employed appear to be men I can trust. They
are certainly fine, brave fellows.

10 *But there is one thing I have not been able to find,*
Margaret. I have no friend. When I am glowing with the
enthusiasm of success, there will be no one to share my joy;
if I am disappointed by failure, no one will be there to offer
me any sympathy.

15 *I shall write everything down, it is true, but that will be*
a poor way of expressing my feelings. I need the company
of a man who will share my hopes and dreams.

Perhaps you will think I am too romantic, my dear sister,
but I feel very sad that I have no friend. I have no one near
20 *me who is gentle yet brave, well educated and intelligent,*
and whose interests are like my own. Here, there is no one
to encourage me with my plans, and help me perfect them.

Such a friend would greatly help to improve the faults of
your poor brother! I am too anxious to get started on things,
25 *and too impatient when there are difficulties. But the worst*
thing about me is that I have not had a good education.
For the first fourteen years of my life, I did whatever I liked.
I read nothing except our uncle Thomas's books about
famous voyages. It was only when it was too late for me to
30 *learn easily that I realized the importance of studying*
foreign languages. Now I am twenty-eight and I know less
than many schoolboys of fifteen. It is true that I have thought
more then they have, and that my ideas are more extended
and more magnificent than theirs, but these ideas need
35 *developing, and I greatly need a friend who will encourage*
me and guide me in this.

Well, my complaints will do me little good. I shall certainly find no friend on the wide ocean, nor even here in Archangel, among merchants and seamen.

I cannot properly describe to you my feelings, now that our expedition is almost ready to start. It is impossible to give you a true idea of that trembling sensation, half pleasant and half fearful, that seems to run through my whole being. I am going to unexplored regions, to the land of mist and snow, and that is very exciting for me.

I will tell you a secret. I have often thought that my great interest in going on a voyage of exploration has something to do with the poems we read when we were children. There seems to be, inside me, something that I do not understand, driving me towards this. In a practical sense, I have always been a hard worker, and a careful one, too — but besides this I seem to have a special love for the marvellous and the unusual. It affects everything I do. Now it is pulling me away from the common pathways of men and out to the wild and unvisited regions that I am about to explore.

But to return to dearer thoughts: shall I meet you again, after having travelled across immense seas and returned by the most southern parts of Africa or America, dear Margaret? I dare not expect to be so successful, yet, at the same time, I cannot bear to think about failure.

Continue for now to write to me whenever you can. Perhaps I shall receive your letters at a time when I need them most to encourage me. I love you very dearly. If you never hear from me again, remember me with affection.

Robert.

Letter 3

At sea, 7th July

My dear sister,
I am quickly writing a few lines to say that I am safe and well, and on my way to the North Pole. This letter will

reach England on a merchant ship which is now sailing
home from Russia. I am in good spirits, and my men are
brave and loyal. They are not at all frightened by the huge
sheets of ice that we see floating past us every day. We are
5 already very far to the north, but the winds from the south
breathe warmth over us, which I had not expected.

So far, everything has gone wonderfully well. I will not
take any foolish risks, but I am more than ever determined
to succeed.

10 Heaven bless you, my sister,

Robert.

Letter 4

At sea, 5th August

My dear sister,

15 A very strange event has taken place. I must keep a written
record of it, even though there is no way, at the moment,
of sending these letters to you.

Last Monday we were almost completely surrounded by
ice. It had closed in on us from all sides, and there was
20 hardly any water in which the ship could float. Things were
beginning to look dangerous, especially as we were also
surrounded by a very thick fog. We decided to wait patiently
and hope for a change in the weather.

About two o'clock, the mist cleared away. We could see
25 huge and uneven plains of ice stretching out in every
direction. They seemed endless, and some of my companions
groaned with despair. I too, was beginning to be worried,
when a strange sight suddenly attracted our attention. We
saw a vehicle moving quickly across the ice, drawn by dogs
30 — a sledge. It was about half a mile away and heading
northwards. The driver who guided the dogs had the shape
of a man, but was as tall as a giant. With our telescopes,
we watched the speedy progress of this traveller until he
disappeared behind some distant slopes.

We were absolutely amazed by this sight. As far as we knew, we were many hundreds of miles away from any land. Several of the men wanted to follow his tracks, but I refused to give them permission. It would have been far too dangerous.

About two hours after this event, we heard the sea move beneath the ship. Before night the ice broke and we were free. However, we decided to remain where we were. It was dark and we were afraid of crashing into huge masses of ice which were beginning to float all around us. I took advantage of this delay and went to rest for a few hours.

The following morning, as soon as it was daylight, I went up on deck and found all the sailors crowded on one side of the ship. They were talking to someone in the sea. I looked down and saw a sledge, similar to the one we had seen the day before. It had floated towards us during the night on a large piece of ice. Only one of the dogs was left alive. Inside the sledge, however, was a human being. The sailors were trying to persuade him to come aboard our ship.

This man was a European. He did not look anything like that other traveller we had seen the day before. As I approached, the first mate said, 'Here is our captain. He will not allow you to die in the middle of this sea.'

5   *As soon as he saw me, the stranger spoke to me. 'Before I come on board your ship,' he said, 'would you please tell me in which direction you are going?'*

I was amazed by his question! When the ice melted, this man would sink and drown beneath the deep, cold waters!

10   *I would have thought the first thing in his mind would be to get onto our ship. However, I told him we were headed towards the North Pole. Upon hearing this, he seemed satisfied and agreed to come aboard.*

15   *Good God, Margaret! If you could have seen this man, you would have been as shocked as I was. He looked dreadful! His arms and legs were frozen and his body was almost a skeleton. I have never seen a man in such a terrible*

20 *condition. We carried him below into a cabin, but as soon as he was removed from the fresh air, he fainted. We had to carry him back onto the deck. There we restored him to life by forcing him to swallow a small amount of brandy.*

Next we wrapped him up in blankets and placed him near the chimney of the kitchen stove. Gradually he recovered and had a little soup.

Two days passed before he was strong enough to speak. I had great trouble stopping the men from bothering him 5 *with their questions. One, however, asked him why he had come so far over the ice in his sledge.*

The stranger's face became very sad and he replied, 'I must find the one who runs away from me.'

'Was he travelling on a sledge, like yourself?' 10

'Yes,' he replied.

Then we told the stranger about the giant we had seen. This made him very excited and he asked us many questions. He wanted to know in which direction 'the demon', as he called him, had set off. He wanted to know if I thought the 15 *breaking up of the ice might have destroyed the other sledge. He kept wanting to go up on deck to look for signs of wreckage, but we forced him to remain inside, as his health was still very bad.*

Since then the stranger has gradually improved, but he 20 *is very silent. When anyone except myself enters the cabin, he seems to be anxious, as if he expects to hear some bad news. Yet he is so caring and gentle that the sailors are all interested in him, and I, myself, begin to love him as a brother. His deep grief fills me with sympathy. He must have* 25 *been a very noble creature in his better days.*

I said in one of my letters, my dear Margaret, that I would find no friend on the wide ocean; yet now I have found a man who in happier times, I would have gladly called the brother of my heart. 30

13th August

The stranger and I have become friends. He is a gentleman and comes from a good family. All the crew admire him. During one of our conversations, he asked me why I wanted to find the North Pole. I told him how I had a hunger for 35 *adventure and knowledge. I told him that I was prepared* to sacrifice my fortune and my entire life, if I could only discover something about the strange and mysterious world in which we live. One man's life or death were but a small price to pay, I said, for knowledge that would give human society power over the forces of nature.

As I said this, the man's face suddenly became filled with great sadness. He covered his eyes with his hands, and tears began to fall through his fingers. A groan burst from his body. 'Unhappy man!' he said. 'Do you share my madness? Hear me — let me tell you my tale, and you will give up your dreams forever.'

I was very curious about what he might tell me, but he was so full of sadness that he became ill, and it was not for many hours that he was able to speak again.

When he felt better, he asked me first to tell him about myself. The tale was quickly told, but I mentioned my desire for a friend, and told him how sure I was that without one good friend, no one could be truly happy

'I agree with you,' replied the stranger. 'Unless we have someone wiser, better, dearer than ourselves to help us improve — a true friend ought to be such a person — then we are only half complete. I once had a friend, the most noble of human creatures, and I know something about friendship. But we are not the same. You, Walton, have hope and the world before you. I have lost everything, and cannot begin my life all over again.'

His face showed such calm sadness that my heart was touched. But he would say nothing else, and presently went back to his cabin.

But I must tell you, Margaret, that although he is so sad, no one can enjoy more deeply than he does the beauties of nature. The starry sky, the sea, and every other wonderful sight in these northern regions seem still to have the power of lifting his soul from earthly cares. Such a man has a double existence. He may suffer misery and great disappointment, yet, when he sits quietly and alone, he will be like a heavenly spirit whose heart is entirely free of sorrow and selfishness.

Will you smile because I have so much to say about this god-like wanderer? You would not, if you saw him. I know that you would value the extraordinary abilities of this wonderful man.

Sometimes I wonder what it is about him that makes him 5 *seem more attractive than anyone else I have ever known. I believe it is his natural intelligence, his quick but never-failing power of judgement, and his clear understanding of the causes of things — this and the pleasant, easy way he has of expressing his ideas.* 10

19th August

Yesterday the stranger said to me, 'You can see, Walton, that I have suffered great misfortunes. I decided at one time that the memory of these evils should die with me, but you have persuaded me to change my mind. You are searching for 15 *knowledge and wisdom as I once did, and I hope that your wishes will not harm you as much as mine have harmed me. I do not know if telling you my story will be of any help to you; yet, when I see what you are about to do, I imagine that you may learn something from my unhappy* 20 *experiences. Prepare yourself, then, to hear of happenings which are usually called "marvellous".'*

I thanked the stranger for his kindness. With his permission, I am to write down the details of his story whenever my duties allow. As I write, his voice seems to ring 25 *in my ears. I can see his eyes and his thin hands trembling with emotion. In some ways he reminds me of a ship that has been wrecked by a fierce storm. His story must be a truly strange and terrible one, for it to have caused him so much suffering.* 30

THE EARLY LIFE OF VICTOR FRANKENSTEIN

Childhood

My name is Victor Frankenstein. I was born in Switzerland and my family was rich and very respectable. It may seem strange, but my childhood was very happy. My parents loved
5   me deeply. They looked upon me as an innocent and helpless creature who had been sent to them from heaven.

For a long time I was their only child. Then we moved to Italy. It was there that my mother met a family of peasants. They were starving and could not afford to feed all their
10   children. My mother looked at the boys and girls very closely. They were all dark-skinned, except one. This was a little girl with beautiful golden hair and blue eyes. My mother wanted to adopt her, and after some thought, the peasant woman agreed. She said the child was not her own. The girl's mother
15   had died when she was born. Her father was an Italian nobleman. He had been arrested for fighting against the government, and now no one knew where he was. He might be in prison, or he might be dead. He had given his daughter to this family so that they would look after her.

20   When my father returned to the house, he was delighted. The girl was called Elizabeth Lavenza and from that time on she lived with us. We all loved her. To me, she became like a sister — but more than a sister. We called each other by the name of cousin, and she was my beautiful and well-loved
25   friend in all my pleasures and interests.

When a second son was born — my brother Ernest, who is seven years younger than me — my parents gave up their wandering life and we went to live at our house at Bellerive, near Geneva. Much later another son was born — my brother
30   William. I loved both my brothers dearly, but to me, of all the children in our family, Elizabeth was always the most important.

Elizabeth and I grew up together. She was less than a year younger than me. We never quarrelled or fought. Our two characters were quite different, but that seemed to draw us closer together. Elizabeth was calmer than me, and thought about things more deeply. I was always full of energy. I could *5* work very hard for long periods, and I wanted to understand things more than she did.

Elizabeth liked to read poetry and romantic stories. Our Swiss home was in a very beautiful part of the country, close to the mountains and lakes. It was calm in the silence of *10* winter, wild and full of excitement in the storms of summer, so there was much to see that delighted her imagination. And while she thought about the appearance of things, I spent my time trying to understand their causes. I looked upon the world as a great secret, and I wanted to know what that *15* secret was. My curiosity about the hidden laws of nature, and the joy of learning to understand them are amongst my earliest memories.

At school I did not have a large number of friends; I preferred to be very close to just a few. My best friend, *20* especially, was Henry Clerval, the son of a merchant in Geneva. He was extremely clever and imaginative. He enjoyed adventure and danger. He loved reading books about the brave heroes of the old times, and wrote stories and plays about them. *25*

I was very eager to learn, but I wasn't interested in history or languages. I wanted to know the secrets of heaven and earth, and understand them: whether I examined the appearance of things, or thought about their inner spirit, the questions in my mind were always about their cause. How *30* did these things come into being? What made them the way they were?

Henry, meanwhile, occupied himself with the moral relations of things, with good and bad, right and wrong. The busy stage of life, the virtues of heroes, and the actions of *35* men were his special interest. His hope and dream was to become famous as a brave adventurer who would do something good for all of mankind.

Elizabeth encouraged us both. Her saintly soul shone out like a lamp in our peaceful home. Her sympathy was ours, her smile, and her soft voice. The sweet look of her eyes was ever there to bless us. Without her I might have become bad-mannered and rough, putting my interests before everything else. Even Henry would not have been so thoughtful and kind, in his passion to become famous, if Elizabeth had not shown him the real loveliness of giving. It was Elizabeth who made the doing of good the true purpose of his love of adventure.

The ideas of Cornelius Agrippa

My interest in science was the main thing which shaped my life, and which set me on the path to my present miserable condition. It all began so innocently.

One day, when I was still a boy of thirteen, we were staying at an inn near Thonon, on holiday. The weather was bad and I had nothing to do, so I began looking around the house, which was very old. I found a book by Cornelius Agrippa. I had never heard of this writer before, and turned over the pages rather carelessly at first. But my feelings soon changed. Agrippa has much to say about the wonderful things that can be found in nature, and he gives many examples and explanations about their causes. I soon became very interested, and very excited. It seemed that this book would help me to understand all the things I wanted to know.

I ran to my father and told him what I had discovered, but he just looked at the title and told me not to waste my time.

If he had explained that the ideas of Agrippa had all been proved false, and that no one believed them any more, and that the methods of modern science were real and practical and could be relied on, then I would have thrown the book to one side and continued with my former studies. Perhaps, even, I would never have thought of the thing that led to my ruin. But I believed my father did not really know much

about the book, and I continued to read, my excitement
growing all the time.

When we got back to Geneva, I read other books by this
writer and other old thinkers. Modern science did not interest
me. The famous Sir Isaac Newton said he felt like a child
picking up shells beside the great and unexplored ocean of
truth, and those scientists that followed him were like mere
beginners. It seemed to me that they simply looked at things
and gave names to them. They could not tell me about what
caused them. The old writers, I thought, could tell me much
more about the true secrets of nature.

It may seem surprising that nowadays anyone would want
to study books which had been written three or four hundred
years before, but although I went to school in Geneva and
was educated in all kinds of modern studies, whenever I
could spare the time, I read about these old scientists.
Agrippa and his friends became my teachers. They started
me thinking about how to turn ordinary metal into gold and
silver. I also began to search for a kind of medicine that
would make people live forever. If only this could be
possible!

I became interested in magic. I muttered strange rhymes
and tried to raise ghosts and devils from the world of the
dead. Elizabeth was horrified by all this. She did not want
to know the secrets of nature. She was only interested in the
beauties of nature. She spent most of her time reading poetry
or walking through fields and gazing at the loveliness of the
snow-capped mountains.

One day, a violent and terrible thunderstorm shook our
house. This event was to change my life. Quite suddenly it
got very dark, and loud bursts of thunder seemed to be
coming from all over the sky. The noise terrified Elizabeth,
who was outside in the garden, and she ran back into the
house. I stood by the door and watched. I was filled with
curiosity and excitement. Suddenly, a stream of fire seemed
to explode out of an old and beautiful oak tree twenty yards
away. Then, when that bright dazzling light vanished, I
noticed that the oak had disappeared. Nothing remained but

a large lump of wood, blackened
and smoking. Next morning we had a
closer look at the tree. Most of it had been
torn into pieces. I had never seen a thing that had once been
5   so large, so completely destroyed in just a few seconds.

   At the time a great scientist was staying with us. He talked
to me about electricity, and the way it effects all living things.
This was quite new to me. As a result, I began to realize that
Agrippa and the old thinkers could not help me. They knew
10   nothing of electricity, and it would be quite impossible to
learn the secrets of nature from them. I gave up my interest
in science completely, and decided to study mathematics,
instead.

   When I think about it, it seems to me that that I had made
15   the right decision. I had turned away from something that
was false and bad, and taken up something true and good.
But no man can escape his fate. I believe, now, there was
nothing I could had done to avoid what happened later on.
Whatever I did, I would not be able to escape the complete
20   and terrible destruction of my life and happiness.

Masters of the world

It was arranged that I should continue my studies at Ingolstadt University, but just before I went there, my mother died. This was to be the first of many dreadful events which were to poison my life. 5

Elizabeth had caught a dangerous kind of fever. My mother looked after her like an angel, and the girl's life was saved. But two days later, my mother became sick with the same illness. She was soon very weak, and we could do nothing to help her. On her deathbed, she made Elizabeth 10 place her hands in mine.

'My children,' she said, 'I had hoped so much to see you married to one another. That, I know, is something your father looks forward to very much. It is the one thing that will make him forget his sadness when I am gone. Elizabeth, 15 my love, it will now be your task to look after Ernest and William. I am so sad to be taken from you, but my hope is that I shall meet you again in another world.'

She died peacefully, soon after she had said these words.

The sadness and emptiness felt by those who have lost a 20 loved one through death is almost impossible to describe. At first one cannot believe that the brightness of a beloved eye, the sound of a voice so familiar and so dear, has gone for ever. Then the actual bitterness of grief begins. But after a time, the sadness slowly passes, and we return to our normal 25 duties once more.

Several weeks after my mother died, the day came once more for me to set off for Ingolstadt. My father was there to bless me. My boyhood friend, Henry Clerval, had wanted to come with me, but he was unable to persuade his father to 30 let him continue his education. Sadly, he shook me by the hand. And Elizabeth begged me to write to her as often as possible. My heart was filled with a sweet kind of sadness as the coach took me away from the happy place of my childhood. 35

Much later, after a long and tiring journey, I saw the high, white steeple of the main church in the town of Ingolstadt.

I stepped out of the coach and was taken to the rooms which were to be my study and my home while I stayed there.

I was not very happy at the university. One of the science professors, Professor Krempe, told me I had been completely wasting my time reading the books of Agrippa. He said that I would have to start all over again, and he wrote down a list of several books for me to buy. He said he would start giving some lectures on natural science the following week, and that another professor, Mr Waldman, would be teaching chemistry.

I was not too disappointed by what the Professor had said. I had already come to think that the old science was useless. I was not sure that I wanted to learn anything more about science at all, and I did not bother to attend Professor Krempe's lectures.

However, out of curiosity, I went to listen to Mr Waldman. He was about fifty years old and had a kind-looking face. He was small but his body was straight, and his voice was one of the most pleasant I had ever heard. To this very day I can hear the words he spoke in a lecture on modern chemistry. 'Times have changed,' he said. 'These days we know that ordinary metal cannot be turned into gold. We know that there is no way to make anyone stay young for ever. Modern scientists spend all their time in a laboratory gazing through microscopes or staring into test tubes. This may seem very dull and unromantic, but they have been wonderfully successful. They have found out how nature works. They now know how to fly right up into the clouds in their balloons. They have discovered how the blood flows around the body. They know all about the air we breathe. Modern scientists have become the new masters of the world.'

That night I could not sleep. I kept hearing the words of Mr Waldman again and again. So much had already been achieved by science, but I, Victor Frankenstein, would achieve much more. I would become an explorer in this new world of modern science, and I would discover the secret of life itself!

The secret of life

I worked very hard. For two years I studied day and night, and my understanding of science increased rapidly. At the end of two years I was able to improve some of the chemical instruments we used, and I became well known in the   *5* university as a good worker.

I was especially interested in living things. I wanted to know what caused them to become alive. In order to obtain human bodies for my experiments, I went into graveyards at night and dug up corpses. I was not afraid. Stories about   *10* ghosts and demons had never worried me in the slightest. As far as I was concerned, a churchyard was simply a place where dead bodies were buried. I felt great pity for those people whose beauty and strength had been turned into food for worms, but that did not stop me. Night after night I examined dead bodies; I examined their eyes and their brains.

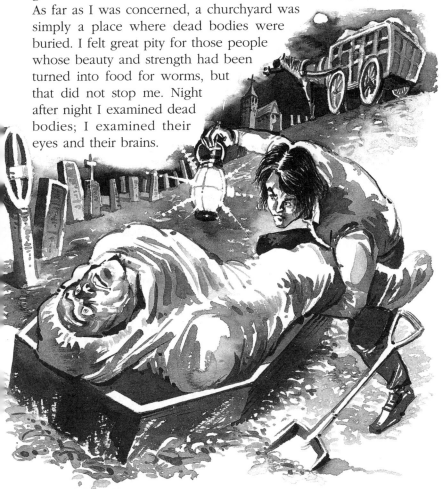

Then, one day, I suddenly understood what had until then been a great mystery. It was an idea so brilliant and wonderful, and at the same time so simple, that I became dizzy with astonishment. I had finally managed to discover the secret of life itself!

I can see by the surprise in your eyes and your eagerness that you too hope to learn that secret. But I will never tell you. Such knowledge has destroyed my life. I will not allow it to destroy yours.

I had discovered the great secret, and, even more exciting than that, I had learned how to create living things from dead material. Now all I needed to do was to build a body that would receive the precious gift of life.

This was to prove difficult. The human body is extremely complicated. There are so many different organs, muscles and veins. Some parts are so tiny that it is very easy to make mistakes, and for this reason I decided to build a body which would be much larger than the usual size. I spent several months collecting my materials, and then I began.

I worked very, very hard. I felt that I was doing something wonderful for the world in which I lived. A new race of human beings would bless me for having created them. I imagined that one day I might even be able to bring the dead back to life.

In fact, I was working too hard. Soon I began to look pale and weak. My body wasted away from lack of proper food and exercise. Time after time I failed, but I kept on trying. Often I would work all through the night, with the moon gazing down on me. Sweat poured from my face as I went about my task. Can you imagine the horrors I had to face as I dug about in damp graves? I worked my own living self almost to death, in order to bring dead matter to life. My arms and legs began to tremble. Even now, my head goes dizzy as I think of some of the dreadful things I did.

But nothing, no matter how horrible, would stop me. I kept working harder and harder. I visited burial places and tore the bodies apart, showing no respect for the dead. I collected bones and pieces of flesh and kept them in a room at the top of the house where I lived. This was my workshop, and I filled it with all kinds of horrors. I obtained my materials from laboratories where medical students cut up corpses and even from places where animals are killed for meat.

As I worked, the summer passed me by. It had been the most beautiful season. The harvest was magnificent and the trees and bushes were full of sweet fruit. But my eyes were blind to the charms of nature. I even stopped thinking about my friends who were so far away from me, and whom I had not seen for such a long time. I knew my family were worried about me. My father wrote me a letter. In it he said, 'I know that while you are pleased with yourself, you will think of us with affection and we shall hear regularly from you. But we have not received a letter from you for a very long time, and I am afraid that can only mean you are not happy with what you are doing.'

Every night I was ill with a kind of slow fever. My eyes ached, and I became so nervous that the slightest sound made me jump. I avoided the company of my fellow men as if I were some sort of criminal.

At times I became frightened of the wreck I had become. I prayed that my work would soon end so that I could take some proper exercise and have time for a little amusement. Only then would I become my normal self once more.

3

THE MONSTER

A living nightmare

On a stormy night in November, I finally finished my task. The body was built. I collected all my instruments around me so that I might bring life to the creature that lay stretched
5   out in front of me. I worked harder than I had ever worked before. I tried again and again to bring the dead mass to life, but nothing happened.

It got very late. At one o'clock in the morning, everything was quiet except for the sound of rain being blown against
10   the windows. My candle was nearly burned out, but I would not stop working. Then, suddenly, in the dim light, I saw the dull, yellow eye of the creature open! The creature breathed hard and a tremendous shudder moved all through its body.

15   How can I describe my feelings when this happened? How can I describe the wretch I had created? His body was perfectly shaped, and I had chosen the different parts carefully so as to make him beautiful.

Beautiful! Great God! The experiment
20   had taken so many months that I had not been able to preserve certain parts of his flesh.

His yellow skin hardly covered the workings of the muscles and arteries beneath. His hair was shiny, black and long. His teeth were as white as pearls. But this beauty only formed a more dreadful contrast with his watery eyes, his loose, wrinkled skin, and his straight, black lips. 5

My feelings suddenly changed. For two years I had worked like a slave in order to bring such a creature to life. Now that I had finished, the beauty of my dream vanished. My heart was filled with horror and disgust. I could not bear to look at the being I had created. 10

I rushed out of the room. For hours I just walked backwards and forwards in my bedroom. A thousand twisted thoughts swept through my mind. My sufferings were so great that I fainted upon my bed. Even then, I was disturbed by the wildest dreams. I thought I saw Elizabeth. She looked 15 very beautiful, walking in the streets of Ingolstadt. Delighted and surprised, I threw my arms around her. But as I pressed the first kiss on her lips, they became black with the colour of death. Her face seemed to change, and then I thought I held the corpse of my dead mother in my arms. A funeral sheet covered her body and I saw worms from the grave crawling in the folds of the cloth.

I woke in horror. A cold dampness covered my forehead and every part of my body began to shake. The dim, yellow light of the moon forced its way through the shutters into my room. It was then that I saw the miserable monster I had created standing close to me. He was holding up the curtain that was drawn around my bed, and what were supposed to be his eyes were looking straight at me. His jaws opened and he muttered strange, meaningless sounds. An awful grin wrinkled his cheeks.

I leapt from my bed. Perhaps he spoke to me, but I was too horrified to listen. He stretched out a hand as if to catch me but I got away from him and rushed downstairs.

I spent the rest of the night in the courtyard next to the house. I walked up and down it for hours. I was frightened and worried, and full of horror at what I had done. Every time I heard a noise, I looked around me, expecting to catch sight of that demon-like corpse to which I had given the gift of life.

No human being could look upon that dreadful face without feeling ill! Even the oldest corpse brought to life could not be so ugly. I had often looked at him while I was putting him together. He had been ugly then, but when the spark of life had flowed through him, he had looked like a creature who had come straight from hell. Worst of all, I had made him a giant. He was about eight feet tall and must surely possess tremendous strength.

During the night, my heart was beating so quickly I could feel every vein and artery inside me bursting with blood. At other times I was so exhausted and weak I almost fell to the ground. Apart from being horrified, I was also bitterly disappointed. All my hopes and dreams had suddenly turned into nightmares, and I felt so ashamed.

A friend arrives

Morning came. It was wet and miserable. My tired, aching eyes could see the church of Ingolstadt, with its white steeple and clock. It was six o'clock. The watchman opened the main gates of the building where I lived, and I hurried out. I raced through the streets, expecting to meet that creature at every corner. I did not dare go back to my rooms. Rain began to pour down from a black and comfortless sky.

I had no idea where I was going. I did not care. I just looked straight ahead, and kept walking. I dared not look behind me because I was afraid I might see the monster following me.

At last I came to the inn in the centre of Ingolstadt where the coaches usually stop, and I noticed that the coach from Switzerland was just at that moment coming along the road. I waited to see who would get off; and there, as the door opened, I saw my old school friend, Henry Clerval. 5

'My dear Frankenstein,' he said, 'I am delighted to see you, but whatever is the matter? Your clothes are all wet, and you look so ill.'

I told him that I had been working too hard and had got caught out in the rain. I was so glad to see my friend. All 10 the memories of my home and family that he brought with him made me so happy that, for a moment, I forgot about the horror of my work, and my misfortune. For the first time in many months, I felt calm. I welcomed Clerval warmly, and after I had asked him about my father, my brothers and 15 Elizabeth, I invited him back to my rooms at the university. As we walked together, we talked about our friends in Switzerland. Henry told me that he felt very pleased because his father had finally agreed to let him study at Ingolstadt.

When we reached the place where I was staying, however, 20 I began to tremble violently. Perhaps the creature was still walking about in my rooms. I was frightened of meeting him again, myself, but I was even more worried that Henry might see him. I told my friend to remain at the bottom of the stairs and I rushed up to my rooms. I put my hand on the lock of 25 the door and then hesitated. A cold shiver ran down my back. Then I threw open the door quickly, like a child who expects to see a ghost on the other side. But there was nothing there. I stepped in quietly and looked around. The place was empty. I could hardly believe my good luck. I 30 clapped my hands for joy and ran down to Clerval.

All through breakfast I kept jumping up and down, clapping my hands and laughing out loud. I was so glad that the creature had gone. Of course, I could not tell Henry the reason for my behaviour; he just thought I was very happy 35 that he had come to Ingolstadt. At first Clerval was amused, but when he looked at me more closely he saw a strange wildness in my eyes, and he became worried.

'My dear Victor,' he cried, 'what is the matter, for God's sake? Don't laugh like that. You seem to be quite ill! What's the cause of all this?'

'Don't ask me!' I screamed, putting my hands in front of my eyes. For a moment I thought I saw the dreaded monster glide into the room like a ghost. 'Oh, save me! Save me!' I cried. I was sure that the monster had come and grabbed me. I struggled furiously and fell down in a fit.

That was the beginning of a long illness. I had a nervous fever, and had to remain in bed for several months.

During all that time Henry looked after me. He did not tell my relations how ill I was. He was worried it might shock my sick and aging father, or cause unnecessary suffering to the tender-hearted Elizabeth.

News from home

I recovered some months later. When I looked out of my window, I saw that the winter was over. It was spring time. The trees were covered with young, green leaves and the world looked very beautiful. I immediately began to feel better, and I was almost able to forget the dreadful memory of that living nightmare I had made. Soon I was as cheerful as I had been before I began my studies at Ingolstadt.

I realized then that I owed my life to Henry. He had given up all his time to look after me.

In my fever I had been forever dreaming about the monster I had made, and I had kept muttering and shouting out about him. Henry must have been very surprised to hear what I said. At first he thought this behaviour was just the effect of my fever, but later, as the subject of my mad words never changed, he began to think something strange and terrible had happened.

One day I said to him, 'Dearest Clerval, how kind and very good you have been to me. This whole winter, instead of studying, which is what you came here to do, you have spent your time looking after a sick man. How shall I ever repay you?'

'You will repay me by staying calm, and getting better as fast as you can,' he replied. 'But there is one thing I would like to talk to you about, if I may.'

I was immediately troubled to hear this. What could Clerval wish to discuss with me. Was it about that one subject that I dared not think about myself?

'Be calm,' said Clerval, who had noticed my discomfort. 'I will not talk about it if it upsets you; but your father and cousin would be very happy if they received a letter from you in your own handwriting.'

'Is that all, dear Henry? But how could you think my first thoughts would not fly towards those dear, dear friends whom I love so much?'

'Well, if that is the way you are thinking, my friend, you will perhaps be glad to see this.' And he handed me a letter from Elizabeth. This is what Elizabeth wrote:

My dearest Victor,

I have learned from Henry that you have been very ill. Nothing would have stopped me from coming to see you, except that I know Henry is so very reliable and I trust him completely. He tells me you are getting better now, so I am sending you this letter.

Get well and return to us soon, dear Victor. We are all happy and cheerful here but we miss you a great deal, especially your father.

The scenery around the house has not changed. The blue lake and the snow-capped mountains are as beautiful as ever.

I know you would be very pleased if you could see how well Ernest has grown up. He is now sixteen, full of energy, and a true Swiss. He dreams always of being a soldier, but we cannot let him go; not, at least, until his older brother comes back to us. My uncle is not very happy about letting Ernest join the army, but Ernest never did have your ability to study. He likes to spend all his time in the open air, climbing the hills, or rowing on the lake. I fear that if we do not let him go, he will become very lazy.

Do you remember Justine Moritz, whom my aunt, your mother, brought to our house when she was twelve, to work as a serving girl? She grew up with us, and your mother, who liked her greatly, made sure that she was given a very
5 *good education. Justine loved your mother in return, and tried her best to copy the way she spoke and behaved. She was very sad when your mother died, but even more sadness awaited her. One by one all her brothers and sisters died at about that time, and just before you went to Ingolstadt she*
10 *had to leave us because there was no one to look after her mother. Well, sadly, Madame Moritz, her mother, died too at the beginning of this last winter, and now Justine has returned to us. She has grown up to be a very clever, gentle young woman, and is extremely pretty.*
15 *I must also say a few words to you about my cousin, the darling little William. He is very tall for his age and has blue eyes, and dark eyelashes. His cheeks are rosy with good health. When he smiles, everyone loves him. He already has one or two little girlfriends, but Louisa Biron is his favourite.*
20 *She is a pretty girl, five years of age.*

Please give our thanks to Henry for his kindness and his many letters. We are sincerely grateful. Goodbye, dear cousin. Take care of yourself and write — just one word will be a blessing to us.

25 *Elizabeth.*

I wrote back immediately. Two weeks later I was able to leave my room and return to the university.

A short holiday

My first thought, when I felt better, was to introduce Henry
30 to some of the professors. Seeing him with me, many of them tried to encourage him to join me in my scientific work. However, by this time I had developed a hatred of science. I could not bear to enter a laboratory, and the sight of any chemical equipment made me tremble with fear.

My professors, including Mr Waldman, kept praising me. They told me I was the most brilliant scientist the university had ever produced. They wanted me to continue with my studies, but I refused.

Henry noticed how much I now disliked the subject. He had, in any case, never enjoyed science, and had already decided that he wanted to study languages. I was easily persuaded to join him.

Three months later, I decided I was strong enough to return home, but I did not go immediately. I was delayed by one or two small matters, and then, when I was ready to go, winter arrived and travelling became impossible. So I passed another winter in Ingolstadt, this time very cheerfully in the company of my good friend.

In May of the following year, shortly before I was due to leave, Henry suggested that we go on a short walking tour. I agreed with pleasure, and we spent two weeks walking through the hills and forests of the countryside around Ingolstadt.

This short holiday did me a great deal of good. Before, my studies and my passion for science had caused me to shut myself away from my fellow creatures. Now my friend Henry Clerval brought out my better feelings. He taught me once more to love nature and the cheerful faces of little children. What an excellent friend he was. I slowly returned to being that happy creature who, a few years before, had loved and been loved by all, and had had no sorrows or cares. The weather was beautiful. Everyone that Henry and I met seemed full of life and happiness. I was so excited and cheerful that, on the day we returned to Ingolstadt, I raced my friend back to the college.

Throughout this time I had seen no sign of the monster I had created. I never spoke to Henry about what I had done — I was too ashamed — and gradually the memory of that dark period of my life began to fade away. I did not realize then what dreadful events were soon to happen, and that this happy and peaceful year was to be the calm before the storm.

Despair

When we got back to the college, I found the following letter
from my father

My dear Victor,

5   *Soon you will be coming home. You will expect to see us
happy and smiling. Instead you will see us full of sorrow.
Something dreadful has happened to us, and you must
prepare yourself to receive the shock.*

William is dead. That sweet child who was so happy and
10   *gentle is dead. Victor, he was murdered!*

*I know it will not be possible to comfort you, but I feel
you ought to know what happened.*

*Last Thursday, I, my niece, and your two brothers went
for a walk along the lake. It was a beautiful evening. We*
15   *walked further than we had planned, and it began to grow
dark before we thought of returning home. It was then that
Elizabeth and I realized that Ernest and William were
nowhere to be seen. They had been walking ahead of us, so
we sat down to rest and waited for them to come back. Not*
20   *long afterwards Ernest returned alone, and asked us if we
had seen his brother. They had been playing, it seemed, and
William had run off somewhere to hide. Ernest had looked
everywhere for him, and waited for him for quite a long
time, but he had not reappeared.*

25   *This rather worried us, and we began to search. Night
came, and Elizabeth thought he might have gone back to
the house, so we returned home. He was not there. I was
worried that my dear little son might suffer from the cold
night, so we decided to go back with torches to the place*
30   *where Ernest had last seen him. Elizabeth was in a state of
shock, and I told her to stay at home.*

*Then, at five o'clock in the morning, I discovered my
youngest son. Just a few hours before he had been happy
and full of health. Now he lay stretched out on the grass.*
35   *His body had changed colour and he did not move. The
marks of the murderer's fingers were on his neck.*

We took the body home. My face was so sad that Elizabeth guessed the truth. She wanted to see the body. At first I refused to allow this, but she insisted. She entered the room and examined the neck of the victim. Then she cried out, 5
'Oh God! I have murdered my darling child!'

She fainted and for a while we feared for her life. When she recovered, she began to weep and sigh. She told me that during the evening of the murder, William had persuaded her to let him wear a valuable locket which contained a portrait of your dear, dead mother. The locket has gone, and this, no doubt, was what tempted the murderer to do his frightful deed. We are making every effort to find the killer, but this will not bring poor William back to life! Come to us, dearest Victor. You are the only one who can comfort Elizabeth. She weeps all the time and blames herself for the death of the boy. Her words are breaking my heart. Thank God your dear mother did not live to see the cruel, miserable death of her youngest child!

Come to us, Victor, but do not come with thoughts of hatred and revenge towards the murderer. Come with feelings of peace and gentleness. You must heal the wounds in Elizabeth's mind, not make them worse.

Your loving father,

Alphonse Frankenstein.

Clerval watched me read this letter. He was surprised to see my face turn from joy to despair. I threw the letter on the table and covered my face with my hands. 'My dear Frankenstein,' exclaimed Henry. 'Why are you so unhappy? My dear friend, what has happened?'

I pointed to the letter and walked up and down as Clerval read it.

'I can't offer you any comfort,' he said after a time, putting the letter down. 'Nothing can bring little William back to life. What do you intend to do?'

'I will go instantly to Geneva. Come into town with me,
Henry, to order the horses.'

During our walk, Clerval did in fact try to say a few words
of comfort. 'Poor William!' he said. 'The little boy is now with
his mother. How dreadful that such an innocent child should   5
feel the cruel grasp of a wicked murderer! Poor little fellow!
We have only one comfort. He is at rest. His pain is over,
his sufferings are at an end forever. The grass covers his
gentle body and he knows no more of the sadness of this
earthly life. We need pity him no longer. Instead, we must   10
show our pity for those who loved him and are still alive.'

Clerval spoke these words as we hurried through the
streets. The words impressed themselves in my mind and I
remembered them later, when I was alone. As soon as the
horses arrived, I hurried into a carriage and said goodbye to   15
my friend.

4

THE TRIAL

The murderer is seen

My journey home was very sad. At first I wanted to get to my relatives as quickly as possible. Then I began to slow down as I got nearer to my home town. I was feeling very confused. I was frightened and I did not know the reason why. I stopped by the side of the lake and stared at it for hours.

Night began to fall. I could hardly see the dark mountains and I felt more and more depressed. I felt there was evil all around. It seemed as if I was to become the most miserable of all human beings. Alas! I was right in every way but one. I could not at that time imagine one hundredth part of all the unhappiness I would experience.

It was completely dark when I arrived outside the town of Geneva. The gates were shut, so I had to spend the night in a small village about a mile away. I tried to sleep but I felt restless. As the sky looked peaceful, I decided to visit the spot where poor William had been murdered. I took a small boat and began to row across the lake. As I did so, I noticed flashes of lightning around the top of Mont Blanc. It was a strange and beautiful sight. The storm came closer and closer. I landed and climbed up a small hill to watch. It moved nearer and nearer. The heavens were covered with clouds. I felt the rain coming in large drops. It fell slowly at first, then it became faster and more violent.

I began to walk back to the boat. The darkness and the storm increased every minute. Thunder burst with a terrific crash over my head, and echoed through the mountains. My eyes were dazzled by bright flashes of lightning. The lake was lit up and looked like a vast sheet of fire. Then for a moment everything went black until my eyes recovered from the effects of the flashes. As is usual in Switzerland, the storm seemed to explode in different parts of the sky all at the same moment.

This magnificent war in the sky made me clench my fists with excitement. I opened my mouth and shouted out aloud, 'William, my little brother! This music in the sky is your funeral song. The gods are sad and angry because of your death!'

As I said these words, a tall figure appeared from out of the darkness. I stood absolutely still and watched with horror. I could not be mistaken. A flash of lightning lit up this being, and I saw its shape clearly. It was the size of a giant and the face was horribly deformed. I knew at once that it was the terrible demon to whom I had given life. What was he doing there? Was he the murderer of my brother? The minute that idea come into my mind, I realized it was the truth. My blood froze and I felt weak and faint. I was forced to lean against a tree for support. Then the figure passed by me quickly and I lost sight of it in the darkness.

He was the murderer! I could not doubt it. I thought of chasing the monster but I knew I stood no chance of catching him. There was another flash of lightning. I saw the creature climbing up the steep rocks of a nearby mountain. In no time at all, he reached the top and then disappeared over the other side. I stood there, motionless. It was as if I had been turned into stone.

The thunder and lightning stopped but the rain continued to pour down, and everything around me was in total darkness. In my mind I began to think about many things that until then I had tried to forget; everything that had happened which led to the creation of that dreadful being, of the appearance of the work of my own hands at my bedside, and its sudden departure. Almost two years had passed since the night that that demon had first been brought to life. Was the murder of William the first of his crimes? I knew then that I had let loose into the world a merciless, evil being, who enjoyed killing and misery; had he not murdered my own brother?

No one could ever know the unhappiness I felt through the rest of that night. I was out in the open air the whole time, cold and wet. But it was not the weather that worried me. My mind was imagining unending scenes of horror and misery. I felt that this creature was like an evil spirit, which had been set free from the grave and was now going to destroy everything that I loved.

A double misfortune

Day came. I found the boat and rowed back across the lake. Soon I was walking through the open gates of Geneva towards my father's town-house. I wanted to tell everybody about the murderer and organize a search party. Then I thought about the story I would have to tell the police. Would they believe that I had met a monster at the foot of a mountain? Would they believe that I had created this monster myself? I remembered the nervous fever that had kept me in bed for several months. They would just say I was ill.

They would lock me up in a madhouse and I would stay there forever. Even if they sent out a search party, they would never catch the monster. Who could possibly catch a creature capable of climbing steep cliffs and mountains? Thoughts such as these made me decide to say nothing.

It was about five o'clock in the morning when I entered my father's house. I told the servants not to disturb the family and went upstairs to the library. Over the fireplace, there was a picture of my mother kneeling by the coffin of her dead father. Below this was a small picture of William. My eyes became wet with tears and a cold shiver crept down my back.

Presently Ernest entered. He tried to smile at me, but I saw that his face was filled with sorrow.

'Welcome, my dearest Victor,' he said. 'What a pity you couldn't have come earlier, when William was still alive and the house was filled with joy. I hope you can comfort Elizabeth. She keeps blaming herself for the death of William. However, now that the murderer has been discovered — '

I was amazed. 'You have found the murderer! Good God! how can that be true? Who could have caught him? It's impossible. It would be like overtaking the wind or trying to stop a mountain stream with a dam made of straw. I saw him too. I saw him in the mountains last night.'

Ernest stared at me and shook his head. He acted as if he thought I was still sick. 'I don't understand you,' he said, 'but what we have found out makes us more miserable than ever. No one would believe it at first, and even now Elizabeth will not be convinced. Indeed, who could ever believe that Justine Moritz, who was so friendly and so fond of all the family, could have been capable of such a dreadful crime?'

I was horrified. 'Justine Moritz!' I cried. 'It must be a mistake. I don't believe it, Ernest!'

My brother shook his head sadly. 'No one did at first, but several facts have now been discovered that make us think she was the one who killed William. Her own behaviour has been so confused, which causes everyone to suspect her even more. She is to be tried later today.'

He told me that the morning on which the murder of poor
William had been discovered, Justine had become very ill.
She had been forced to stay in bed for several days. During
this time, one of the servants happened to move the dress
the girl had worn on the night of the murder. As she did so,
the locket that William had worn around his neck fell from
it. The servant showed this to one of the others who, without
saying anything to anyone in the family, immediately went
to the police. They charged her with the murder, and arrested
her. Justine could not explain anything, which made things
worse. Everyone began to think she had murdered the boy
in order to rob him.

This was certainly a strange tale, but it did not change my
mind at all. I replied earnestly, 'You are all mistaken; I know
the murderer. Justine, poor, good Justine, is innocent.'

My father came in. I saw that his face was filled with
suffering and sorrow, and I knew that the shock must have
come close to killing him. But he tried hard to greet me
cheerfully. I did not wish to talk to him about what had
happened, but Ernest, before I could stop him, said, 'Good
God, Papa! Victor says that he knows who murdered poor
William.'

'We do, too, unfortunately,' replied my father, 'though I
wish I had never learned that so much wickedness could
exist in someone I liked so much.'

At that moment Elizabeth entered the room. She had
grown into a very lovely woman since I had last seen her.
She greeted me with the greatest affection.

'Your arrival, my dear cousin,' she said, 'fills me with hope.
You perhaps will know how to defend my poor, guiltless
Justine. I am as sure of her innocence as I am of my own.
Our misfortune is now twice as hard for us. Not only have
we lost William, that lovely darling boy, but now this poor
girl, whom I sincerely love, is to be taken away from us too.
If she is found guilty and condemned to death, I shall never
be happy again.'

'She is innocent, my Elizabeth,' I said, 'and I am quite sure
of it. Do not be afraid.'

'How kind and generous you are!' Elizabeth said.
'Everyone else believes in her guilt, and that has made me
so sad. I know it cannot be possible, but seeing everyone
else against her has made me lose all hope that we can save
her.' She wept.   5

Tears came into my eyes, but I remained silent. What
could I say? I could not tell her about the monster. She would
not believe me. Nobody would believe me. They would lock
me away in a madhouse. Really, there was nothing I could
do to help that poor girl.   10

My father took Elizabeth's hand. 'If the girl is innocent,'
he said. 'She will be found not guilty at the trial. We will do
everything we can to make sure of that.'

These words calmed me, too. In my own mind I knew
Justine was innocent. I was sure that no jury would hang an   15
innocent woman. All the same, I was sick with worry.

'I am innocent'

We all went to Justine's trial. I felt that I was being tried
myself, and my thoughts caused me immense pain. Would
the result of my curiosity and experiments cause the death   20
of two of my fellow human beings? One was just a smiling
little boy full of innocence and joy, killed by the awful
creature I had made. The other would die in an even more
dreadful way. Everyone would think of her as the wicked
murderess of poor William, and as I knew she was innocent,   25
that would make her death even more horrible. Before this
happened, Justine was such a sweet, happy girl who could
certainly expect to live a happy life. Now all this was going
to be destroyed, and I was the cause. A thousand times I
would have preferred to say that I was guilty of the crime,   30
but everyone knew that I was away from Geneva when
William was killed. If I said such a thing, people would not
believe me.

Justine was very calm. She looked over towards my family
and tears seemed to fill her eyes. She was beautiful, but all   35
the people watching hated her.

She explained what had happened on the night of the murder. She told the court that she had spent that day with an aunt. On her way back to my family home, she had met a man who told her that a young boy named William had been lost. She spent several hours looking for him, and when she tried to enter the town of Geneva, the gates were shut. She spent the night in a barn. Next morning a peasant woman found her wandering about the place where the child had been murdered. She said that she knew it looked suspicious, but she was innocent.

Justine could not explain why the locket was found in her dress. She could not understand why the murderer might put it there. She did not know why anybody should want to destroy her.

She looked at the jury. 'I am innocent,' she said, 'as God is my witness.' Then she wept.

Several witnesses were called upon to speak. They were people who had known her for many years. But they were frightened to say anything good about Justine, because they saw that everyone hated her.

Elizabeth was furious when she saw this, and demanded to speak. 'I am the cousin of the murdered child,' she said, 'but I cannot stand by and watch this girl die just because her so-called friends are cowards. I have known Justine Moritz a long time. She is a kind and gentle girl who loved the dead child deeply. I cannot believe that she killed him. Why on earth should she have wanted to steal that locket? 5 It is not very valuable. If she had wanted it, I would have given it to her gladly.'

The spectators clapped when they heard Elizabeth's speech. They admired her kindness and generosity. But they continued to hate Justine. They still thought she was a 10 murderess. They were disgusted that the girl should be so ungrateful. They wanted her to be hanged, and they shouted out with anger.

That night I could not sleep. I knew Justine was innocent. Had the demon killed my little brother and then found a way 15 of destroying this innocent girl?

Next morning I went back to the court room. My lips and throat were as dry as dust. The jury had come to a decision. Justine had been found guilty, and was to be hanged! Elizabeth came to meet me. 'Justine has confessed to the 20 crime,' she said. 'I will never again believe in human goodness.'

Confessed! I could not believe it! Had I not seen the demon with my own eyes? I felt sure he was the murderer. I took Elizabeth by the hand. 'Listen,' I said, 'there is 25 some mistake. We must go and see the poor girl this very moment.'

The death cell

We entered the gloomy prison cell. Justine was sitting on some straw at the far end. There were chains around her 30 wrists. These chains were also fixed to the wall. I was horrified and disgusted. They were treating her as if she were a wild animal. And tomorrow she would be hanged by the neck until she was dead.

When she saw us, she fell down on her knees and wept. 35 Elizabeth began to cry as well.

'Oh, Justine!' she said. 'Why did you do it? I was so sure that you were innocent. Why did you kill that poor little child?'

'Do you really believe I killed him?' cried Justine. 'Are you going to join my enemies and see me crushed in body and soul?' Her voice was choked with sobs.

Elizabeth was shocked. 'Why did you confess?' she asked. 'The judges might not have condemned you to death if you had not done so.'

'I did confess,' wept Justine, 'but I confessed a lie. Ever since I was put in this prison, the priest has tormented me. He told me I was a monster. He made me so confused I almost believed him. He said that I must confess otherwise he would make sure that I would be forced out of God's church and that I would burn forever in the fires of hell! What could I do? I had no friends. I was sick with a fever. I told a lie. I confessed. And now I am the most miserable creature on God's earth.'

Elizabeth began to weep. She begged forgiveness of Justine for ever thinking her capable of the murder. She said she would speak to the judges. She would try to melt their stony hearts with her tears and her prayers.

Justine shook her head. 'I am not afraid of death any longer,' she said. 'God will give me courage. I leave a sad and bitter world. Perhaps one day I will meet poor little William in heaven!'

I walked over to a far corner of the prison. I did not want anybody to see my face. I uttered a terrible groan. This poor girl was going to die, but I could do nothing. I was the true murderer. It was all my fault. A worm was eating away at the centre of my heart. The flames of hell were burning inside my head and nothing would ever put them out.

We stayed with Justine for several hours. We did all we could to comfort the poor girl. In the end, Elizabeth almost had to be dragged away. 'I wish I were going to die with you,' she cried. 'I cannot live in this world of misery.'

Justine tried to be cheerful for the sake of Elizabeth. She brushed away her bitter tears and spoke in a gentle voice.

'Goodbye, Elizabeth, my one and
only friend. May heaven bless you.
I pray to God that this is the last time
you are ever made to suffer. Live and
be happy, and bring happiness to others.'

5

Justine was hanged the following day. Elizabeth's tears
could not soften the hearts of the judges, and all my words
failed to make them change their mind. Justine had died and
I had killed her!

Later I was to see my father and Elizabeth shed tears upon
the graves of William and Justine. These were the first victims
of my evil experiments.

10

THE RETURN OF THE DEMON

A walk in the mountains

I began to avoid people. I would row into the middle of the lake and let the boat drift there for hours. The only sounds I heard were those of the bats flying across the water, or the frogs by the shore. At times I wanted to jump into the dark and silent waters and end my life there and then. But then I thought of Elizabeth and my father. I had to remain alive. I had to protect them from the evil of the monster. I knew in my heart that the demon would strike again. How I hated that creature! I wanted to take him to the top of the highest mountain and throw him down to his death.

Our house was filled with sadness. My father was very ill, and poor Elizabeth was beginning to have nightmares. She kept dreaming of dreadful beings who thirsted for each other's blood. She felt she was walking along the edges of a pit and thousands of people were crowding around her. In her dream, they kept trying to push her into the pit. She kept seeing herself falling down to her death.

One day, I went for a walk into the mountains. I wanted to try to forget my sorrows. I climbed higher and higher. I saw rivers and fields and ruined castles hanging on the edges of steep cliffs covered with pine trees. Far above me were the snow-capped peaks. They were so beautiful! They seemed to belong to another world, where many mighty gods lived. I watched as avalanches of ice and snow fell downwards with a great roaring sound. Huge rocks and pine trees, broken like match sticks, were swept along and fell with a crash into some deep valley.

I walked up dangerous, slippery pathways. I saw mists and clouds and fields of ice. I had never climbed so high in my life. I had never seen such beauty. I took a deep breath and shouted out with joy and triumph.

As I did so, I suddenly noticed the figure of a man. He was some distance away, but coming towards me with super-human speed. He jumped over huge cracks in the ice and climbed over great rocks as if they were stepping stones. He was much taller than any ordinary human being. I could not move. A mist came over my eyes and I felt faint, but the cold air of the mountains quickly brought me back to consciousness. I saw the figure more clearly now. It was the demon. It was the monster that I had created! I trembled with rage and horror as I waited for him to come closer. I decided that I would fight him to the death!

The creature came near. I was surprised to see that his face was filled with deep sorrow, pain and bitterness. It was an unearthly sight, almost too horrible for human eyes to look upon. But I took little notice of this. At first I was speechless with anger and hatred, and when I had recovered, my fury was great indeed. 'Devil!' I shouted. 'Do you dare come near me? Don't you fear my revenge? Come closer, you horrible creature, and I will throw you down into the dust and kick the life out of you. If only your death could bring back to life those you have murdered!'

The demon stopped. Then he spoke. His voice was deep and clear. 'I expected this,' he said. 'All men hate the unfortunate; how much then must I be hated, I who am more unfortunate than any other living thing. Yes, even you, my creator, hate me and want nothing to do with me. Look at me, Frankenstein. I am the ugliest of all things in this world! I am hated by everyone. You must help me. If you do not, I will continue to kill and destroy wherever I go. I will spill the life-blood of all those you love. None will escape me.'

'You monster!' I yelled. 'The tortures of hell are too good for you. Yes, I created you. Now I will destroy you!'

My anger gave me tremendous courage. I sprang on him. I wanted to tear him to pieces, but he was too quick for me. It was like trying to catch a shadow.

'Stop!' he said. 'You must hear what I have to say. I am far stronger than you. I could easily kill you, but I will not hurt you. I am your creature. You gave me life. You are my

God. You should treat me with kindness and understanding. You have treated me as if I were the Devil, when it is you who have made my life a living hell. Everywhere I go, I see a happiness I cannot share. I was once kind and good, but misery made me bitter and evil. Frankenstein, make me happy, then I shall once again be a better creature.'

'No!' I yelled. 'I will not listen to you. We are enemies. We must fight to the death.'

Again I tried to catch him, but again he escaped.

'Will you not listen to me?' he cried. 'Is there nothing I can say that will make you look on me with kindness? Believe me, Frankenstein, I was once gentle. My soul once glowed with love and friendship. But am I not all alone, now; miserably alone? You, my creator, hate me, so what hope   5
have I that anyone else will accept my love? I am hated! I am hated by all men. Everywhere I go, I am hated. I am forced to live in these deserted mountains. I am forced to sleep in caves of ice. My life is truly wretched. Man is now my enemy. Should I not make him as miserable as he makes   10
me? I will destroy thousands. I will become a whirlwind of rage against people. Only you can save them. Listen to my story, Frankenstein. You must let me speak in my own defence. You accused me of murder, yet you want to murder me. You would murder the creature to whom you gave   15
life. How can you, my creator, have no feelings of pity for me at all?'

I covered my eyes with my hands. 'I curse the day I created you,' I shouted. 'Go away! I never want to see you again.'   20

'Come with me,' insisted the demon. 'My story is long and strange. Come to the hut up on the mountains. The sun is still high in the sky. Before it sets behind those cliffs of snow and lights up another part of this earth, you will have heard all that I have to say. With your help I could lead a harmless   25
life from now on. Without it I will become a bloodthirsty killer. I will destroy all those you love.'

As he spoke, he led the way across the ice. I followed. My heart was filled with misery and fear. But I was curious. I wanted to hear his story. I wanted to find out whether or   30
not he had killed my brother. Also, much of what he had said was true. I was responsible for this creature. Shouldn't I try to help him? Wasn't it my fault he was so wicked?

We crossed the ice and climbed up a huge rock. The air was cold and the rain began to fall. We entered the hut. The   35
demon was full of hope, and I was thoroughly depressed. But I agreed to listen to him. He lit a fire, and we sat down beside it. Then the monster began his story.

Early memories

'I find it difficult to remember the first few weeks of my life. Everything was so misty and confused. I could see, hear, feel and smell, but it was hard for me to distinguish one thing
5   from another. At first I remember seeing a very strong light which made me shut my eyes. Then there was darkness. But soon after this there was light again, and this time I found I could walk, and I believe I can also remember moving downwards.

10   'I soon noticed something new about my sensations. To begin with, I had only been able to see shadows and shapes, but not long afterwards, I found I could see things that I could walk around, or climb over.

'As I walked, the light became stronger and stronger, and
15   the heat began to worry me. I looked for somewhere where I could shelter from the light and the heat, and wandered off into the forest near Ingolstadt. I lay down by the side of a stream to rest. Then I was tormented by hunger and thirst. I ate some berries which I found hanging on the trees or
20   lying on the ground. I drank water from the stream. Soon afterwards I fell asleep.

'It was dark when I awoke. I felt cold and frightened. I was all alone in a strange world. I had covered myself with some clothes before leaving your house, but these did not
25   protect me from the damp of the night. I was a poor, helpless, miserable creature; I knew nothing and had no idea where I was; my body seemed to feel pain on all sides. I sat down and wept.

'Then I noticed that a gentle light had come into the sky.
30   It filled me with pleasure. I stood up and watched this bright, glowing form rise from among the trees. I stared at it with a kind of wonder. It moved slowly, but it lit up my path, and I set off in search of berries.

'There were no clear ideas in my mind. Everything was
35   still confused. I felt light and hunger and thirst and darkness. Hundreds of sounds rang in my ears, and I noticed smells of different kinds coming from all around me. But the only

object that I seemed to know was the bright moon shining in the sky, and I stared at that with pleasure.

'Several days and nights passed. I began to see things even more clearly. I could see the stream from which I drank and the trees which shaded me with their leaves. Then I heard the sweet sounds of song. These came from the throats of the little winged animals which kept flying about in front of my eyes. Sometimes I tried to imitate the pleasant song of these creatures, but I was not able to do so. Sometimes I felt I wanted to express myself in my own way, but the strange noises that came from my mouth frightened me into silence.

'My eyes became better and better. I could now see insects and flowers. My hearing improved, too. I could hear the sound of birds clearly. I learned that the sparrow could only make a sharp sound, but the blackbird's song was sweet and musical.

'One day I felt very cold. Then I found a fire which had been left by beggars. I was overcome with delight at the warmth that I could feel coming from it. In my joy I put my hands into the flames. The next moment I pulled them out again with a cry of terrible pain. This I could not understand. But I looked carefully at the fire to see how it was made, and learned to heap wood upon it to keep it going. When night came, I found out with pleasure that the fire gave out light as well as heat. Then I found some small pieces of food that the beggars had roasted. They tasted delicious.

'But food became scarce. I often spent the whole day looking for a few nuts to satisfy my hunger. One day I decided to leave that place, and I set off across the wood in the direction of the setting sun. Three days passed, and at length I discovered the open country. There had been a great fall of snow the night before, and the fields were a clear white. This filled me with sadness. My feet were cold from walking through the snow.

'It was about seven o'clock in the morning, and I longed to find food and shelter. At last I saw a small hut which had been built for a shepherd. This was a new sight and I looked at it with great curiosity. The door was open, so I went in.'

The monster meets some people

'There was an old man inside the hut. He was sitting by a fire cooking his breakfast. He turned round on hearing a noise. When he saw me, he gave a loud shriek and dashed
5 out. I watched him running away across the fields at tremendous speed. I was astonished. I had never seen that form of living creature before, and I could not understand why he ran away from me. What was the matter with him?

'However, I was delighted with the hut. Here the snow
10 and rain could not enter. The ground was perfectly dry. I felt I had found myself a home. I greedily ate what was left of the shepherd's breakfast. This consisted of bread, milk, cheese and wine. It was delicious, apart from the wine which I did not like. Then I was so tired, I lay down on some straw
15 and went to sleep.

'It was noon when I awoke. The sun was warm and shone brightly on the snow-covered ground. I decided to travel on. I put some food into a bag and walked across the fields for hours. By sunset, I arrived at a village. I had never seen a
20 village before. How beautiful it seemed to me! There were small huts, cottages and a few large houses. I saw vegetables in the gardens. There was milk and cheese in the windows of some of the cottages. I became curious. I entered one of the largest houses. When I did so, the children began to
25 scream, and one of the women fainted. All the people in the village came out to see what was happening. When they saw me, some ran away in terror and others attacked me. They threw sticks and stones at me, and anything else they could find. The stones that hit me hurt very much.

30 'I escaped and ran away across the fields. Frightened, I found a small hut in a garden and hid in it. It was a miserable-looking place, compared to the well-built homes I had seen in the village. It joined on to a neat, pleasant-looking cottage, but after what had happened, I did not dare
35 to go in there.

'Early next morning I got up and examined my new living place. It was only about four feet high. It was so small that

I hardly had enough room to sit up in it. It was made entirely
of wood. There was nothing on the floor, which was just
bare earth, but it was dry. There were many cracks and small
holes in the walls which the wind whistled through, but I
found it a good enough place to sit in, away from the snow   5
and the rain. Here, then, I stayed, happy to have found a
shelter, both from the bad weather and the unkindness of
man.

'I blocked up the doorway to the hut with stones and
wood so that no one would know that I was living there.   10
Next, I covered the floor with some straw, and I began to
eat a loaf of bread which I had managed to steal. I was
happy. This place was paradise compared to the cold, wet
forest with its damp earth.

'Suddenly I heard a footstep. I looked through a hole in   15
the wall and saw a woman pass by with a pail on her head.
She was young and gentle-looking, and had long, fair hair.
She looked quite different from the rough villagers
I had met the day before, but she was
dressed poorly in a jacket made
of some coarse cloth, and a
simple blue skirt. I did not
see where she went, but
in about a quarter of an
hour she came back,
this time carrying the
pail, which was
partly filled with
milk. A young man
came out from the
cottage, and spoke
to her. I did not
know what he said,
but it sounded
rather sad. Then he
took her pail and
they went back into
the cottage together.

'Soon after this, I saw the young man again. He was carrying some tools, and went across the field at the back of the cottage. The young woman also seemed to be busy, sometimes inside the cottage, and sometimes outside in the yard.

'I was very curious. I turned towards the back wall of my hut. There was a small crack in the wood there. I looked through and found that the hut had been built directly in front of one of the cottage windows. To my delight, therefore, I was able to see inside.

'I saw a small room. It was bright and clean, but there was hardly any furniture. In one corner, an old man sat near a small fire. He was leaning his head on his hands, and looked very sad. I watched as the young woman went around the cottage, making it clean and tidy. Then she took some work from a drawer and went and sat down beside the old man. He picked up a musical instrument, and began to play sounds sweeter than the song of any of the birds I had heard. The picture of the old man playing the guitar and the young woman sitting beside him doing her work was a lovely sight, even to a miserable creature like myself, who had never seen anything beautiful before.

'The silver hair and kindness of the old man and the gentleness of the young woman, caused feelings of love and respect to fill my heart. The old man played a sweet, sad tune, and I saw tears on the face of the young woman. He then spoke to her, and she put her work to one side and knelt at his feet. He held her close to him, and smiled at her with such kindness and affection that I began to feel in myself sensations of a strange and very powerful kind. They were a mixture of pain and pleasure such as I had never felt before, either from hunger or cold, warmth or eating good food. I did not understand what was happening to me. After a while I turned my head away, unable to watch any longer: the scene caused such strong emotions inside me.

'Soon after this, I saw the young man walk past my hut, carrying some wood. I turned again, to look into the cottage. I saw the young woman meet him at the door, take some of the wood and place it on the fire. The young man showed her a large loaf of bread he had brought with him, and some cheese. She seemed pleased, and went into the garden for some roots and plants. She placed them in a pot of water which she stood on the fire. Later they all sat down to eat. *5*

'Night came soon after this, but to my surprise I found the cottages could make light through the use of candles, and so the pleasure I experienced in watching them could continue. Once again the old man took up his instrument and began to play. When he had finished, the young man *10* began to make sounds that were quite unlike the old man's music. The other two sat quietly, and seemed to be listening to him. I later discovered he was reading aloud from a book, but at that time I knew nothing about language or letters. I watched all this in amazement. Then the candles went out *15* and the family, I supposed, went to sleep.'

THE MONSTER'S EDUCATION

The unhappiness of the cottagers

'I lay on the straw in my little hut, but I could not sleep. I thought of everything that had happened that day. I remembered very well how the people in the village had treated me, but mostly I thought about the gentleness of those in the cottage. I wanted to join them, but dared not do so. I decided to stay quietly in the hut for as long as I could, so that I might discover as much as possible about them.

'The next day was like the day before. The young man was busy outside the cottage, and the young woman worked inside. The old man, whom I soon realized was blind, seemed to spend all his time playing his guitar, or simply thinking. The two younger ones were very loving and respectful to him, and everything they did for him was done with affection and gentleness.

'They were not, however, completely happy. When the two younger ones thought the old man would not hear them, they would sit quietly at one end of the cottage, weeping. I was very puzzled by this. If such lovely creatures could be miserable, it seemed less strange that someone like myself should also be unhappy. But I could not understand the cause of their unhappiness. It seemed to me they possessed a lovely home, and many other fine things. They had a fire to keep them warm when it was cold, and delicious food to eat when they were hungry. Best of all, they had each other's company to enjoy.

'After some time, I discovered that one cause of their unhappiness was that they were very poor. At first I did not know what this meant, but I began to see that the only food they ate came from their garden, and they only had one cow to give them milk. They were often hungry, and at times the two young ones gave the old man food when they had none for themselves.

'Their kindness to the blind old man greatly affected me. I had been taking vegetables from their garden to eat, but when I found that this made things worse for them, I stopped. Instead I lived on berries, nuts and roots which I got from the forest.

'I was able to help them in other ways, too. I found that the young man spent a great part of each day collecting wood for the family fire. During the night I often took his tools, and went to the forest to get enough firewood to last them for several days. I left the firewood in a pile outside their door. The first time I did this, the young woman was greatly astonished when she opened the door the following morning. She spoke some words in a loud, high voice. The young man came out, and also seemed surprised. It pleased me to notice, later, that he did not go to the forest that day, but spent the time working in the cottage and the garden.

'Sometimes, when there was snow on the ground, I cleared their footpath for them. They thought it was very mysterious that work they usually did for themselves had been done by an invisible hand. I heard them say words like 'wonderful' and 'good spirit'. At the time I did not know what those things meant, but I saw the young people were pleased with what had been done.'

Learning to speak and to read

'One day I realized something about them which I thought was very interesting. It seemed that the sounds they made were their way of communicating experiences and feelings to one another. I noticed that these sounds could cause pleasure or pain, smiles or sadness in the minds and on the faces of those who listened. This was, I thought, a godlike science. I decided that I must learn it.

'At first I found it very hard. Their pronunciation was quick, and often what they said had no connection with anything I could see. However, by listening to my cottagers

as carefully as I could, and by observing them closely, I soon
discovered the words for 'fire', 'milk', 'bread' and 'wood'. I
learned the names of the cottagers. The young man and the
young woman had several names. The young woman was
5 called 'Agatha', or 'sister', and the young man was, 'Felix',
'brother', or 'son'. The old man only had one name, which
was 'father'. At night I went deep into the lonely forest and
tried to imitate the sounds they made, and this way I slowly
began to master their language.

10   'After a time I wanted to show myself to them and to speak
to them, but I knew by then how ugly I was. I had seen my
face in the pool of water beside my hut. I was so unlike the
cottagers that I was filled with anger and shame. But there
was hope, I thought. If I learned to speak like them, and if
I learned to understand their way of
life, perhaps they would not be so
frightened by my ugliness.
Perhaps they could learn to
love me.

'Through listening to their conversations, I learned about the difference between the sexes, and the birth and growth of children. This made me feel sad, because I could not understand where my own friends and relations were. Did I have none? As far as I could remember, no father had ever watched me at play when I was small; no mother had ever blessed me with sweet smiles and kisses. What was I? Where had I come from? I kept asking myself these questions again and again. Everywhere I went I looked around, but I never saw or heard of anything like me. Was I truly a monster? Was this why men threw stones and pieces of wood at me, and ran away from me?

'Sometimes, when there was little to do in the winter evenings, Felix would read to everyone. At first I did not understand what he was doing, but then I noticed that he used many of the same sounds when he read as when he talked. I guessed therefore, that on the thing he was looking at, he could see signs for words. I became very excited when I realized this, and immediately wanted to learn to read. But then I saw how difficult it would be for me, for I did not know what sounds I was supposed to make when I saw the signs.

'Luckily for me, a lady came to the cottage one day. She was on horseback. She was dressed in a dark suit, and her face was covered with a thick, black veil. Agatha came out of the cottage and spoke to her, but all the lady would say in reply was 'Felix'.

'On hearing his name, Felix came out of the cottage. When he did, the woman lifted her veil. I could see then that she was young and very beautiful. Her face was like the face of an angel. She had shining black hair, and dark eyes which were gentle and at the same time full of life.

'Felix was delighted. His face was suddenly filled with enormous pleasure, and all sorrow vanished from it. I could hardly believe he was the same person, the change was so great. His eyes sparkled, his cheeks glowed with pleasure, and at that moment I thought he was as beautiful as the stranger.

'This young woman, named Safie, had come to stay with them. I could see that Felix liked her very much, but I also noticed that Safie could not speak their language very well. I thought this was strange, but, day after day, as I listened to them teaching Safie to speak, I learned as well. This way I made much better progress, and it was not long before I knew their language as well as anyone.

'I learned how to read too. I listened as Felix and Agnes read to the old man and Safie. Then I stole their books and put them back later.

'The more I read, the more I began to wonder who I was and where I had come from. The first book I studied was a history book, called Volney's *Ruins of Empires*. I would not have understood it at all if Felix had not explained it so carefully to Safie. From this I learned about different parts of the world, and about the customs, governments and religions of different nations. I heard about the great old Empires of Asia, Greece and Rome; of Christianity and the modern kingdoms of Europe. I learned about the discovery of America, and wept with Safie when I heard the sad story of what happened to the people who first lived there.

'These stories made me wonder about human beings. Was man really so powerful and magnificent, and, at the same time, so wretched and wicked? From what I read, he seemed at one moment to be the most evil of creatures, and at another the most noble and godlike. For a long time I could not understand how one man could kill another, or why there needed to be laws and governments. But then, when I heard the details of their battles and wars, their cruelty and bloodshed, I turned away in disgust.'

The story of Safie

'Some time passed before I knew who the cottagers and their friend Safie really were. I found out that the old man's name was De Lacey, and that he came from a very good French family. The De Laceys had lived for many years in Paris and had once been rich and comfortable. Felix had worked for the government of France, and Agatha had been like a young and beautiful princess.

'Their lives had changed because of Safie's father. He was a Turkish merchant who lived in Paris and who, for some reason I never learned, got into trouble with the French government. He was arrested and thrown into prison. On exactly the same day, Safie arrived from Turkey: she had come to live in Paris with her father.

'The Turkish merchant was tried and condemned to death. Everyone in Paris thought this was very unfair. It was generally believed the government was punishing him because of his religion — he was not a Christian — and, as he was a rich man, it seemed they also wanted to take his wealth.

'Felix was horrified when he heard about this. He decided to try to help the poor man. He got passports in the name of his father, his sister and himself, and then, after freeing the merchant from prison, he used these papers to help the Turk and Safie escape. They left France and went to Italy.

'In doing this, Felix met Safie and fell in love with her. Unfortunately his actions had also got his whole family into trouble. It became too dangerous for them to live in Paris. They ran away to save themselves, and were now poor cottagers, living near a small village in Germany.

'Safie's father had agreed that she and Felix should be married, but when the merchant heard that the family had lost all its wealth and importance, and were now living the lives of simple country people, he changed his mind. He did not want his daughter to marry a Christian, especially not a poor one. He ordered Safie to forget about Felix, and to return with him to Turkey.

'Safie, however, loved Felix and would not go back to her own country. She found out, by reading some of her father's papers, where Felix and his father and sister were living, and had come on her own to find them and stay with them.

'During this time, Safie had found someone to help her write letters to Felix, and often, in the evenings, I noticed that the young people would take these letters out and read them together. At first I did not understand what they were doing, but I could see the letters were very interesting to Safie and Felix, and that reading them had a marvellous effect on their spirits. Sometimes, when there was no one in the cottage, I got in and made copies. I thought I must learn all about this sort of writing, which affected the emotions of men and women so much. I have the copies of these letters with me. I can show them to you, if you wish, so that you will believe what I am telling you.'

Moments of truth

'The story of my beloved cottagers impressed me deeply. I understood then why they were so gentle, and yet so poor; why they were different from the rough villagers, and why they seemed so sad, until Safie came to live with them. But there were other things I learned which did not please me so much.

'One night, when I had gone to the forest to get them some more firewood, I found on the ground a leather bag. Inside it were some clothes, and some books. I can hardly describe to you the effect these had on me. They gave me much to think about and wonder at, but they also made me feel very unhappy about myself.

'One of the books was a long poem, called *Paradise Lost*. In it I learned how God had created the first man, Adam, and his wife, Eve. I wondered who had created me. I read how the Devil had been thrown into hell. I learned about the Devil, and learned that he and all his followers were ugly. I wondered if they were as ugly as me, or if I was a devil like them.

'One day, I reached into the pocket of the clothes I had taken from your workshop. I found some papers there. Now that I could read, I looked at them with great excitement. They were the notes you made when you were creating me! At last, I thought, I would discover the truth.

'But when I saw that you had made me from pieces of dead bodies, and used your knowledge of science to bring me into this world, I was filled with disgust and anger. "Cursed be the day that I first received life!" I cried. I was filled with agony. I hated the name Frankenstein. Why did you make a monster so ugly that even you turned away from me in disgust? God made man beautiful, but you made me a thing of horror. If you hated me, who could possibly love me?

'I did not give up hope, however. The cottagers were so good and kind. Surely they would not be frightened of my horrid and deformed appearance? After all, they never drove away the beggars that stopped by their door and asked for food. In a few months' time, I thought, I would show myself to them.

'I began to think of Paradise. I imagined the beautiful creatures there, and thought of them showing me love and affection. I saw them smile like angels, and my days were filled with everlasting joy. But it was all a dream.

Unlike Adam, I had no Eve. There was no woman at my side to bring me happiness and comfort. God had given Adam a mate. Where was my god, and why had he not given me a companion? My creator had deserted me, and in my heart I cursed him.

'The months passed by. All this time I was afraid to show myself. I waited until, one day, the blind man was in the cottage alone. Then I decided to speak to him. My heart was beating madly as I walked quietly up to the cottage door. All was silent. I knocked.

' "Who is there?" said the old man. "Please come in."

'I entered. "I am sorry to disturb you," I said. "I am a traveller and I am very tired. Could I possibly stay by your fire for a few minutes?"

' "Come in, come in," said the old man. "I will do what I can to help you, but I am blind. My children are out in the fields and I shall find it difficult to get you any food."

' "There is no need to worry," I replied. "I have some food. It is only warmth and rest that I need."

'I sat down and there was silence. I knew that every minute was precious but I did not know how to begin the conversation.

'The old man spoke. "Do you come from this part of the country?"

' "No. I am from Geneva. There are some people here that I wish to meet. I love them dearly and I hope they will love me."

' "I wish you good luck."

' "These people have never seen me before. They do not know me at all. I am full of fear. If I fail to win their friendship, I will be all alone for the rest of my life."

' "Do not despair. It is terrible to have no friends, but the hearts of men are full of love. Be hopeful."

' "These people are the most excellent creatures in the world. However, I fear that they will be prejudiced against me. I am good. I have never harmed anybody. I have feelings and I am kind, but when they look upon me they will only see me as a terrible monster."

' "That is very unfortunate. But if you have done nothing wrong, cannot you make them believe in your goodness?"

' "That is what I am about to do. That is why I am so afraid. I love these friends with all my heart, but they will believe I wish to hurt them. It is this prejudice that I must overcome." 5

' "Where do these friends live?"

' "Very near here."

'The old man was silent for a moment. Then he spoke. "If you give me all the details of your story, perhaps I could 10 make them believe in your goodness. I am blind and I cannot see your face, but your voice tells me you are sincere. I would be happy to help a fellow human being."

' "Bless you! I accept your generous offer. You have lifted me up from the dust. I hope that with your help, I will not 15 be driven away from human society as if I were a wild and dangerous animal."

' "God forbid!" cried the old man. "That should never happen, not even to a criminal. Such treatment makes men evil and desperate. It is a shocking thing to do to a fellow 20 human being."

' "How can I ever thank you? I have never heard such kindness from the lips of men before."

' "Could you tell me the names of these friends and where they live?" 25

' "I was silent for a moment. This was the most important moment of my short life. I would either be happy or miserable forever. I tried to speak, but the effort was too much for me. I sat down in a chair and sobbed loudly.

'At that moment I heard footsteps. The young people were 30 coming back. I did not have a moment to lose. I grabbed the old man's hand. I cried, "Save and protect me! You and your family are the friends I was talking about. Do not fail me in my hour of greatest need!"

' "Great God!" exclaimed the old man. "Who are you?" 35

'Then the cottage door opened, and the young people entered. Who can describe their horror and amazement on seeing me? Agatha fainted. Safie screamed and ran out of the

cottage. Felix rushed forward and
with the strength of ten men, tore
me from his father, to whose knees
I was clinging. In a fit of rage and hate, he
5   threw me to the ground. Then he struck me violently with
a stick. I could have torn him into little pieces just as the
lion tears apart a young deer. But my heart was filled with
sickness and disappointment and I did nothing. He lifted up
his stick to strike me a second time. I ran out through the
10   door. Nobody saw me escape into the safety of my hut.'

THE MONSTER'S REVENGE

A creature of evil

'How I cursed you, Frankenstein! I cursed you from the bottom of my heart. I wanted to kill myself. I wanted to kill you. I wanted revenge. I could have destroyed the cottage in my hate. I could have torn the cottagers to pieces. I would have enjoyed listening to their screams and their misery. It would have been like a feast.

'When night came, I left my hut and wandered into the wood. There I began to shriek and howl. I was like a wild beast that had broken out of its cage. I raced through the forest, tearing up trees and destroying everything that got in my way.

'That night was filled with misery for me. The cold stars seemed to laugh at me. The bare trees waved their branches above me. Now and then the sweet voice of a bird echoed in the silence. All creatures except me were asleep or happy. I was as miserable as the devil, and I felt as if I were trapped forever in the burning fires of hell. I wanted to destroy the world. I wanted to crush it, or to choke it to death with my bare hands.

'In despair and exhaustion, I fell asleep.

'Next morning the sun rose. I felt refreshed. I realized I had acted like a fool. I should not have shown myself to the rest of the family. I should have spent more time explaining to the old man that I was so terribly ugly to look at. Perhaps it was not too late. I decided to return to the cottage and try once more to win the old man's friendship.

'These thoughts made me feel calmer. In the afternoon I fell into a deep sleep. But the fever in my blood did not allow me to enjoy pleasant dreams. I kept seeing Agatha fainting. I kept seeing Safie running from the cottage, screaming like a madwoman. Again and again I saw Felix pulling me away from his father's feet and beating me with a stick. I woke up exhausted and found that it was already night time. I crept from my hiding place and went back to the hut.

'The sun rose once more. I waited for the family to get up, but all was silent. I trembled. Where were they?

'Presently Felix came into the cottage with a man I had not seen before. I listened carefully to their words.

' "Do you know what you are saying?" said the man. "If you go now, you will still have to pay me three months rent and I shall take all the vegetables in the garden. Wouldn't it be better to wait for a few days and think it over?"

' "No," said Felix, shaking his head. "We will never again live in this cottage. The place is haunted by a demon. My father is in danger of dying from the shock, and my sister and our friend will never recover from it."

'Felix shuddered violently as he said this. He and the other man then left. I never saw any of the cottagers again.

'I spent the rest of the day in the hut. I was filled with despair. I had been deserted. There was now no hope of anyone ever loving me.

'My feelings of self-pity gave way to those of hatred. That night I destroyed all the vegetables in the garden and began to heap wood and straw around the hut. The moon rose out of the sky and a fierce wind blew from the direction of the woods. The clouds were being swept across the sky at great speed. The strength of the wind was as powerful as a mighty avalanche, and my mind was filled with a terrible madness. I lit the dry branch of a tree and danced with fury around the cottage. I waved this torch about my head, and with a wild scream I set fire to the wood and straw. The wind fanned the fire and the cottage was quickly covered with flames. I watched these flames cling to the building and licking at it with their snake-like tongues.

'I had become a creature of evil. And so I decided to start looking for you, my dear Frankenstein. You were the one who had created me. You were the one who had made me into this frightful monster.'

A good deed unrewarded

'It was a long journey to Geneva. I travelled only at night. I was out in the open the whole time and it was bitterly cold. Rain and snow poured around me. The mighty rivers were frozen. The surface of the earth was hard and bare.

'But as I came nearer to Switzerland, the sun became warmer and the land turned to green. One morning, I found that my path lay through a deep wood. I decided to travel on during the daylight. It was spring. The weather was so beautiful that even I felt cheerful.

'As I came out of the woods, I saw a deep and fast-flowing river. The trees were all around and bent their branches into it. Suddenly I heard the sound of voices. I hid behind some bushes and waited. A young girl came running towards the spot where I lay hidden. She was playing hide and seek with somebody. I watched as she ran along the steep bank of the river. Suddenly she slipped and fell into the stream.

'Without thinking, I rushed from my hiding-place. I dived into the waters and caught hold of her. The current was fast and I had great difficulty in dragging her to the shore. The girl was unconscious. She lay upon the grass and did not move. I tried very hard to bring her back to life. As I did so, a farmer appeared. He ran towards me and tore the girl from my arms. Then he raced away into the deeper part of the woods. I followed him. He turned round and aimed a gun at me. He fired and I fell to the ground.

'I watched the man disappear and I clenched my fists with rage. Was this the proper reward for my kind action? I began to twist about on the ground. I was in pain. Part of my flesh and bone had been shattered. All my feelings of gentleness gave way to hellish fury. I ground my teeth and snarled like a wild animal. I was determined to hate the human race for the rest of my life.

'For some weeks after that I led a miserable life in the woods. I tried to cure my wound. The bullet had entered my shoulder and I could not get it out. I promised myself that one day I would have revenge upon my enemies.

'When my wound had
healed, I continued my journey.
Soon I arrived outside the town
of Geneva. I found a place to hide,
5   not far from the lake, and it was there that I fell asleep.
   'Little did I know that my revenge was soon to come.'

The murder

'I was woken up by the approach of a beautiful child. He came running towards the place where I had hidden. He was full of life and energy. As I watched him, an idea came into my head. The child seemed far too young to know anything 5 about the horror of my deformed body. I decided to catch him and keep him. I would teach him to become my friend and companion just as a man teaches a dog to love and respect him.

'With this in mind, I grabbed him as he went past. The 10 moment he saw me, he placed his hands before his eyes and uttered a shrill scream. I dragged his hands away from his face. "Do not scream," I said. "I don't wish to hurt you. Listen to me."

'He struggled violently. "Let me go," he cried. "Monster! 15 Ugly beast! You wish to eat me and tear me to pieces. Let me go or I will tell my father."

' "Boy," I said, "you will never see your father again. You must come with me."

' "Let me go, monster! My father is a very important man. 20 He is Mr Frankenstein. He will catch and punish you. You had better let me go."

' "Frankenstein!" I snarled. "Then you are a relative of my hated enemy. You will be my first victim."

'The child continued to struggle. He kept on calling me 25 names and insulting me. My heart was filled with despair and anger. I squeezed his throat to silence him. In a moment he lay dead at my feet.

'I looked down on my victim. His neck and face had turned blue and his tongue hung from his mouth. My heart 30 swelled with joy and triumph. I clapped my hands. I shouted out, 'I too can cause suffering and death. It is the turn of my enemy to feel pain. I will have my revenge. The life of Frankenstein will not be worth living.'

'As I fixed my eyes on the child, I saw something glittering 35 on his chest. I took it. It was a locket on a gold chain, with the portrait of a most lovely woman. For a few moments I gazed with delight on her dark eyes and her lovely lips. But presently my rage returned. I reminded myself that such a creature would never love me. If she ever saw me, she would scream and her face would become ugly with disgust and fear. At that moment, I wanted to rush upon the town and tear every living person in it to pieces.

'Suddenly I felt tired. I needed rest. I left the spot where the murder had been committed and looked for a better hiding-place. I entered a barn, thinking it was empty. Inside, I saw a woman sleeping on some straw. She was young and beautiful. I wondered if she could ever love me. I bent over her and whispered, "Awake, my beauty. Your lover is near. I would give up my life if you would just give me one kiss."

'She stirred in her sleep. I was terrified. Would she really wake up? Would she curse me? Would she afterwards find the dead child and let the world know that I was a murderer? But she did not wake up. Then a hellish idea came into my mind. I decided that she should be punished for my crime. 5 I bent over her and placed the locket in her dress. She moved again and I ran away.

'For some days, I haunted the spot where the murder had taken place. Sometimes I wanted to see you and sometimes I wanted to kill myself and put an end to all my sufferings 10 for ever. At length I wandered towards these mountains. I have travelled all through their deep valleys. I am filled with a burning wish that only you can do something about. You will never be rid of me until you have given me this one thing. 15

'Listen to me, Frankenstein, my creator. I am alone and I am miserable. You must make me a woman. She must be as deformed and ugly as myself! She alone will not run away from me in terror. She will be my companion and my wife! You must do this for me, because I am your creature and 20 you must help me!'

The promise

The monster stopped speaking and looked at me. He was waiting for a reply.

'I refuse,' I said. 'And no torture in hell shall ever make 25 me change my mind. I shall never create another creature like you. Two of you together might destroy the whole world with your wickedness.'

'Listen to me,' replied the demon. 'I am only wicked because I am unhappy. If you had your way, you would 30 throw me off a cliff into a valley of ice and you would not call this murder. Why should I pity my victims if they don't pity me? If you don't help me, I will destroy everyone who comes within my reach. I will do everything in my power to make you miserable. I will make you wish you had never 35 been born.'

The demon trembled as he spoke. He was filled with a horrible rage and his face twisted into all sorts of frightful shapes. But after a moment he calmed himself down and continued speaking. 'You are the cause of my sufferings and my crimes, Frankenstein. You know that I am not asking for too much. My demands are quite reasonable. All I want is a woman who looks as ugly as myself. I know we will both be monsters. I know we will be cut off from the world. That will not bother us. We will be happy with one another. We will lead a harmless and happy life far away from the places human beings inhabit. Have pity on me, Frankenstein! Don't refuse me!'

I took a deep breath. I was beginning to feel sorry for the monster I had so foolishly created. He was intelligent and sensitive. He had all the feelings of a normal human being. Should I try to make him happy?

The demon continued. He was very persuasive. 'If you agree to do this,' he said, 'neither you nor any other human being will ever see me again. I will go into the vast jungles of South America. I do not eat the same food as man. I do not have to kill sheep or cattle to fill my stomach. I can live off nuts and berries. My companion will be the same. We shall make our bed of dry leaves. The sun will shine upon us and ripen our food. We shall live a life of peace.'

'How can I be sure?' I said. 'You may return to the world of men. You may try to win their kindness and their love. Once again they will hate you and try to destroy you. Then you will surely become angry again. And you will have a companion who will help you to murder all who stand in your way.'

The monster gave a groan. 'Now you are torturing me,' he said. 'Why should I return to the world of men? I will live in complete happiness with my wife. Why should I return to those who hate me?'

His words had a strange effect on me. I felt sorry for him. I even wanted to comfort him. But when I looked at that filthy mass that walked and talked, I felt sick. I knew my feelings would change to horror and hatred. This made me feel guilty. It was my fault that he was so ugly. I had no right to prevent him from being happy.

'You promise you will do no harm to anyone,' I said, 'but how can I trust you? Perhaps this is just a trick. Perhaps you just want more power so that your revenge can be all the more terrible.'

'You must trust me,' he said. 'If I have a companion, I will bless my maker. I will be at peace with mankind. I will once again become kind and gentle. If I am to remain alone, I will get worse and worse. I will make the world suffer. I will make the world as miserable as myself.'

I said nothing. I was thinking. Perhaps the monster would become kind and good if he had a companion. If I did not agree to help him, he might well become a murdering madman. He could live in caves of ice. He could climb huge mountains as if they were tiny hills. Nobody would ever be able to catch him or track him down. He could attack towns and villages and murder anyone whenever he wished. I decided that it would be better to help this creature.

'I agree to help you,' I said, 'on one condition. You must swear to leave Europe forever. You must swear to leave every place inhabited by man. If you agree to do this, I will give you a female who will go with you.'

'I swear by the sun and the blue skies of heaven,' he cried, 'if you make me this female, you will never see my face again. Now you must go home and begin your work. I shall keep a check on your progress. When you and my woman are ready, I shall appear.'

Then he left me. I saw him go down the mountain faster than an eagle. He disappeared amongst the hills of ice.

I had spent a whole day listening to this story. The sun would soon fall below the mountains. I began to walk down, back towards Geneva. But my heart was heavy and my steps were slow. All the time I kept thinking about the promise I had made to the monster. Soon night fell, and I had to find a resting place.

I sat down beside a fountain. Every so often the clouds were swept away and the stars shone down upon me. The dark pine trees were all around. Here and there a broken branch lay on the ground. It was so strange and so quiet. I wanted to stay in that spot forever.

Then morning came. I went down to a nearby village but I did not rest there. I went straight to Geneva. I felt as if the weight of the mountains were pressing down upon me. I was in agony. I returned home and showed myself to the family. They were horrified by the strange wildness of my appearance. But I would not answer their questions. I was ashamed of what I had promised to do, and did not feel worthy to speak to them. Yet I loved them. I had to save them. That was why I was going to set about my dreadful work.

But I was worried. Was I doing the right thing? That question kept repeating itself again and again inside my brain. Was I doing the right thing?

FRANKENSTEIN TRAVELS TO ENGLAND

Making a second monster

I found it very difficult to begin the awful task that the
monster had demanded of me. Days and weeks passed by.
I feared the revenge of the disappointed demon, but I did
not have enough courage to make a start. I spent whole days   5
all alone in a small boat in the middle of the lake. I did
nothing but watch the clouds and listen to the sound of the
waves passing by.

It was then that my father told me that I should marry
Elizabeth. He was an old man and did not want to die before   10
this happy event. I loved Elizabeth with all my heart, but I
did not want to marry her straight away. I had to create a
female for the monster first. If I did not, he would seek his
revenge. I told my father that I was planning a trip to
England, and that I would marry Elizabeth when I returned.   15
I needed to go to that country to obtain information which
would help me in my experiments. Also, I knew the monster
would follow me there, and that meant my family would be
safe from his cruelty.

I left Switzerland in September. I was very sad to say   20
goodbye to Elizabeth. Two days later I arrived in Strasbourg.
It was here that I met Henry Clerval again. My father had
asked him to go with me on my long journey. What a contrast
there was between us! He was so happy and full of life, and
I was so depressed.   25

We took a small boat and sailed down the Rhine
through Germany. The scenery was very beautiful. We saw
islands surrounded by willow trees and many small towns.
There were dark, shady woods and vineyards with green,
sloping banks. I lay down in the bottom of the boat and   30
stared upwards at the blue sky. We could hear the songs
of workers in the fields as we glided down the river.

Henry was overjoyed. He felt as if he had been carried away into fairyland.

'I have seen so many beautiful sights in my own country, Victor,' he said, 'but nothing can compare with the charm of this land. When you see such beauty, you know that there is a God in heaven.'

Poor Clerval! Where are you now? Your body lies beneath the soil and the worms eat away at your flesh. Are you in heaven? Your beauty has rotted like the leaves in autumn. I pray to God that your soul is watching over me!

At Cologne we left our boat and travelled by carriage to Rotterdam. Then we journeyed by ship to England. Suddenly my heart was filled with sadness and fear. I had not forgotten the task I had to do. I had not forgotten my promise to the monster, and he had not forgotten me.

Henry and I spent four weeks in London. I visited a number of scientists and obtained all the information I needed. Then I began to collect together all the materials I wanted for my work. I did this in secret. I did not want Henry to know about the horrors of what I was about to do.

I received a letter from Scotland. It came from a friend who had once spent some time with my family in Geneva. He wanted me to visit him in Perth. I accepted this invitation as it fitted in with my plans. I told Clerval I wanted to make the tour of Scotland on my own. I was worried that he might be harmed by the demon.

I left my friend in London and set off on my journey. I did not go to Perth, but to the Orkneys instead — a group of small islands far away to the north of Scotland. There I looked for a lonely place where no one would disturb me.

It did not take me long to find somewhere suitable. I rented a miserable-looking hut. The roof had fallen in and there was no door. I had the hut repaired and I converted it into a place which could be used for my experiments.

Each day my work became more and more horrible. Sometimes I could not bear to enter my workshop for several days. At other times I slaved day and night in order to complete the task. It was a filthy kind of work. When I had first made the monster, I had been excited and full of hope. I had not been too bothered by the horror of what I was doing. Now that I was working against my will, I was filled with disgust. My heart was made sick by the work of my hands.

The scenery of the island made me feel nervous, too. The beach was covered with rocks and stones of various sizes. The waves of the sea roared and crashed against my feet. The land was bare and the cattle looked half-starved. I kept thinking of the beauty of Switzerland with its hills covered with fruit trees and cottages. How different it was from this terrible place! Here the giant ocean roared all day and all night like a spirit from the land of the dead.

As I worked, I was filled with fear. I kept imagining that the demon was watching me all the time. I was sick in my heart and I kept asking myself the same question: 'Am I doing the right thing? Am I doing the right thing?'

Bit by bit, the creature in the workshop was taking shape.

Frankenstein's determination

I sat one evening in my workshop, all alone. The sun had just set and the moon was rising from the sea. There was not enough light to continue working, and anyway I was beginning to have second thoughts about the promise I had made.

Three years ago I had produced a creature who had turned into a murdering monster. This creature had brought misery to those I loved and had filled my heart with sorrow. I was now about to make another such creature. I had no way of knowing how she would behave. She might become ten thousand times more evil than her mate. She might delight in murder for its own sake. She might enjoy torturing people and causing them misery. The demon had sworn to leave the civilized world and hide himself in deserts and jungles where no one might see his face ever again, but she had made no such promise. She might refuse to go with him. The two creatures might even hate each other.

The demon was disgusted by his own ugliness. He might be even more disgusted by the sight of the female I was creating for him. And she might turn in disgust from him. She might be attracted by the superior beauty of man. Then the demon would become even more cruel.

Even if they liked one another, and went into the jungles of South America, there would still be problems. Supposing they had children? They might produce a race of devils who would conquer the world and destroy mankind, or turn them into terrified slaves. The name of Frankenstein would be cursed forever.

I then looked up and my heart almost stopped beating. In the light of the moon I could see the demon.

He was standing by the window. A terrible grin wrinkled his lips. Yes, he had followed me on my travels. He had walked through forests, he had hidden himself in caves. He had been watching me all the time.

His face was filled with trickery and cunning. I knew then that he could not be trusted, and that I had made a terrible mistake! I trembled with fear and anger. I began to tear the creature to pieces with my bare hands. Soon they became covered with blood and pieces of muscle. My fingernails were choked with skin and hair. I almost fainted with disgust and horror.

The demon gave a loud howl of despair and disappeared from the window.

I left the room and locked the door. I made a promise in my own heart that I would never again begin that work. Then, with shaking steps, I went back to my own room, and sat there, alone. There was nobody to help or comfort me.

Several hours passed. I stood by my window looking out at the sea. It seemed almost motionless. The winds made no noise and all nature seemed to be resting under the quiet eye of the moon. A few fishing boats were on the water and I sometimes heard the sound of voices as the fishermen called to one another. Then I heard the sound of oars near the shore. A boat had landed close to my house.

In a few minutes I heard the the noise of my door slowly opening. I trembled from head to foot. I wanted to shout out to one of the islanders who lived in a cottage not too far away, but I was not able to do this. I was frozen to the spot. I was like a child who wants to run away from a nightmare, but finds he cannot move.

Presently I heard the sound of footsteps coming along the passage. The door opened and the demon appeared. He closed the door behind him. Then he came near me. He was snarling with rage. 'You have destroyed the work which you began,' he said. 'What are you trying to do? Do you dare to break your promise? I have suffered great hardships because of you. I left Switzerland with you. I crept along the shores of the Rhine. I was there on its islands and I climbed across the tops of the surrounding hills. I have lived many weeks in the woods of England and in the forests of Scotland. I have often been cold and hungry. You cannot imagine how I have suffered. Do you dare destroy my hopes?'

'Yes, I do. I am breaking my promise. I will never create another monster such as you. I now see you for what you really are, a creature of evil!'

'Wretched slave!' roared the demon. 'I can make your life a living hell. You are my creator, but I am your master. You will obey me!'

'Never!' I shouted. 'Your threats are useless. Do you really think I will create another monster such as yourself?'

The monster saw the determination in my face. He looked very angry. 'In this world, each man has a wife and each beast has a mate,' he snarled. 'Why must I be all alone? Do you think I will allow others to be happy while I am miserable? I will have my revenge. I will wait and I will watch you. Take care, Frankenstein!'

'Do your worst, you spiteful demon! I will never change my mind.'

'Very well,' he said. 'I will go. But remember this: I will be with you on your wedding night!'

I moved forward and tried to catch him. But he was far too quick for me. He raced out of the house with the speed of lightning. A few moments later, he was in his boat. It flew across the waters like an arrow. Soon it was lost amongst the waves.

All was again silent, but his words still rang in my ears. I was burning with rage. I wanted to follow this demon and throw him to the bottom of the ocean.

I walked up and down my room. I was very worried. A thousand terrible nightmares rushed through my mind. I shuddered in horror. Who would be his next victim? Then I remembered his words, 'I will be with you on your wedding night!' That would be the date of my death. The demon would strike and his revenge would be ended.

I was not afraid. Death would be a release from my misery. What angered and upset me most was how Elizabeth would suffer when her husband was snatched away from her on her wedding night. No doubt that was all part of the demon's plan of revenge. I clenched my fists in fury. Let the demon come, I said to myself. When he comes, I will be ready for him!

A body by the sea shore

The night passed away and the sun rose from the ocean. I felt calmer. I left the house and walked on the beach. I wanted to stay on this island forever. If I returned to Geneva, I would be killed. I would see those I loved die in the grasp of the demon. To think that I had created this monster with my own hands!

I walked about the island like a restless ghost. I was lonely and miserable. The sun rose higher in the sky and I became sleepy. I had been awake the whole night and my eyes were red and sore. I lay down on the grass and fell into a deep sleep.

When I awoke, I felt refreshed. Yet the words of the demon still rang in my ears.

The sun was beginning to set when I saw a fishing boat coming towards the island. It landed close to me, and one of the men brought me a packet. It contained letters from Geneva, and one from Clerval. My friend wrote saying that he had to go back to London soon and he wanted to see me as quickly as possible. He was waiting for me in Perth. I decided I would leave the island and join him in two days time.

But before I departed, I had a job to do. I shuddered at the thought of doing it. I had to pack up my chemical instruments. I had to collect them from that hut. The next morning I opened the door of the workshop and looked in. The remains of the half-finished creature lay scattered upon the floor. I almost felt as if I had mangled the living flesh of a real human being. I packed up my instruments. Then I put all the pieces of the body into a basket and filled it up with heavy stones. I had decided to throw everything into the sea

that very night. I did not want the islanders to become
suspicious and horrified by all those pieces of mangled flesh
and bone.

Between two and three in the morning, the moon rose in
5   the sky. I put my basket into a little boat and sailed four
miles from the shore. The sea
was almost empty.

There were only one or two fishing boats returning towards land. I sailed away from them. I felt as though I were about to commit a dreadful crime. I wanted to avoid meeting any of my fellow human beings. Suddenly the moon was covered over by a thick cloud. I took advantage of this moment of darkness and threw the basket into the sea. I listened to the sound it made as it sank below the waves. Then I sailed away as fast as I could.

As I got closer to the shore, the sky became completely covered by cloud, but the air was pure and sweet. It refreshed me and raised my spirits. I decided to stay on the water a while longer. I fixed the rudder to stop the boat from moving. Then I lay down at the bottom of the boat. Clouds hid the moon. Everything became dark. I could only hear the sound of the waves gently splashing against the boat as it moved from side to side. The murmur of the water was like music. In no time at all I was sound asleep.

I do not know how long I was asleep. When I woke up, I had a shock. The wind had become very strong. Large waves were sweeping all around my little boat. I had been driven far from the coast. I wanted to turn back. I pulled on the rudder. To my horror, the waves came leaping over the sides of the boat and almost filled it. I had no choice. I had to let the wind carry me forward like a leaf in a storm. I was frightened for my life. I had no compass with me and so had no idea where I was going. I might be swept into the wide Atlantic ocean. There I would feel the tortures of starvation. The waves grew larger. They roared and smashed against the tiny boat. Perhaps I would be swallowed up by these savage waters!

I had already been out for many hours. I began to feel the torment of a burning thirst. I looked up to the heavens. Fast-flying clouds were racing across the sky. I looked at the sea. Was this to be my grave?

'Devil!' I exclaimed. 'Your revenge has come!' I thought of Elizabeth, of my father and of Clerval. They would be next to suffer from the evil cruelty of the monster. I fell into a daydream of despair and horror.

Hours passed by. The sun began to fall towards the horizon. The wind died away into a gentle breeze. There were no more huge waves upon the sea, but the boat kept moving from side to side. I felt sick. I was too weak to hold
5 the rudder properly. Then, all of a sudden, I saw land towards the south. I was saved!

Tears of joy filled my eyes. Strength came flooding back into my heart. I tore off my shirt and made it into a sail. I could now see trees. There were ships near the shore. I saw
10 a church steeple pointing towards heaven. I sailed into the harbour. I had escaped the anger of the sea.

A crowd gathered round. They watched me pull down the sails. They whispered together. Nobody offered to help me. I looked at them closely. They were frowning. There was
15 hatred in their eyes.

'My good friends,' I said, despite the looks on their faces, 'I am tired and hungry. I have been lost at sea. Will you tell me the name of this town?'

'You will find out soon enough what it is called,' replied
20 a man with a rough voice. 'We have a little room waiting for you.'

I did not understand this rudeness. 'Why do you answer me so roughly?' I replied. 'Is it the custom of Englishmen to be so rude to strangers?'

25 'I do not know about the customs of the English,' snarled the man. 'This is Ireland. And it is the custom of the Irish to hate wickedness.'

The crowd grew quickly. Their faces were full of curiosity and anger. I was worried and annoyed. I asked if there was
30 a place in town where I might find food and rest. Nobody answered. Then I moved forward. The crowd began to murmur. They followed me and surrounded me. A man came up to me. He tapped me on the shoulder. 'Come along, sir. You must follow me to Mr Kirwin.'

35 'Who is this Mr Kirwin?' I said. 'And why should he demand to see me? Is this not a free country?'

'Yes sir,' said the man. 'This is a free country for honest people. Mr Kirwin is a judge. You have some explaining to do. Last night a man was murdered here. We found his body by the sea shore.'

At first I was frightened, but then I grew calmer. I was innocent. This could easily be proved. I followed the man in silence. He took me to one of the best houses in the town.   *5*
I was so exhausted, I almost dropped to the ground. However, I kept on my feet. If I fell down, the crowd would see this as a sign that I was frightened, and they would think I was guilty. I did not realize then what was in store for me. I did not know that I was soon to be overwhelmed by horror   *10*
and despair.

I must pause here. It requires all my strength to tell the rest of this story.

THE MARRIAGE

A dreadful shock

Mr Kirwin was a wise old man. He was pleasant but strict. He asked some witnesses to tell him what had happened.

I learned that three fishermen had found a dead body on the sand. At first they had thought it was the corpse of a person who had been drowned and washed ashore. Then they had looked more carefully. To their surprise the body was dry and still warm. They had carried it to the cottage of an old woman. There, they had tried to bring the body back to life, but they had failed. The corpse was that of a handsome young man. His death had been caused by strangling. All around his neck were the black marks of the murderer's fingers.

When I heard about the marks of the fingers, my mouth fell open with shock. I suddenly remembered the murder of my brother William. My arms and legs trembled. A mist came over my eyes. I was forced to lean against a chair to stop myself from falling. Mr Kirwin noticed this. No doubt he saw it as a sign of guilt.

One of the other fishermen had some more information. He said he had seen a man leaving the shore in a boat just before the body was discovered. He said it was the same boat as the one in which I had just landed.

They all claimed that I was the murderer. They said the storm had probably blown my boat back to the shore. That was why I had not been able to make my escape.

Mr Kirwin listened to the evidence. Then he said I should be shown the dead body. They took me along to a nearby house. I was not the least bit worried. I had been talking to some islanders in the Orkneys on the night of the murder. What had I to fear?

I entered the room where the corpse lay. Then I was led up to the coffin. The lid was pulled back and I was able to gaze down on the face of the victim.

How can I describe my feelings when I saw him? Even now my throat is as dry as the dust of a graveyard. I cannot bear to remember that awful moment. The judge and the witnesses melted before my eyes. They seemed to disappear like a dream. There, in front of my aching eyes, was the lifeless body of Henry Clerval! I gasped for breath and sank to my knees. 'Have I killed you as well?' I cried out loud. 'You are the third, now, to die because of me. How many more will there be?'

My tired body could no longer take such shocks. I began to tremble. I had to be carried from the room and from that moment I was, for a time, totally mad.

Fever

5   I was ill with a fever. I lay for two months on the point of death. My cries were terrible to hear. I called myself the murderer of William, Justine and Clerval. I said I felt the fingers of the demon already grasping my neck. I screamed aloud with agony and terror.

10   Why did I not die? Why did I not sink into that world of everlasting peace? Death snatches away innocent children and turns healthy people into food for worms. Death fills tombs with dust and the smell of rotted bodies. What was so special about me? Why did I not die?

15   But I was doomed to live. Two months later, I recovered my senses. I woke up to find myself in a prison. All around my rough wooden bed were locks and chains, and barred windows. I remembered what had happened, and I groaned out loud.

20   This sound disturbed an old woman who was sleeping in a chair nearby. Her face was rough and hard. There was no pity in her eyes.

'Are you better now, sir?' she said.

'Yes,' I replied, 'but I wish I were dead.'

25   'I wish you were dead, too,' she said. 'All murderers should die.'

How I hated her for saying that! I grew feverish again and then lost consciousness for several hours. When I awoke, Mr Kirwin was sitting by my bedside.

30   'I am sorry this room is so unpleasant,' he said. 'Is there anything I can get you?'

'No. Just let me die. That is all I ask.'

The judge smiled. 'You may soon be set free from this place. I am sure some evidence will be found to clear your

35   name.'

'I am not afraid of death.'

Mr Kirwin nodded. 'I know how you feel,' he said. 'You have been very unlucky. It must be a terrible thing to see the dead body of your best friend and then be accused of his murder. I sympathize with you, Mr Frankenstein.'

'How do you know my name?'

'When you were ill, all your papers and letters were brought to me. I wrote to your family two months ago.'

'Are they safe?' I cried. 'Has anyone else been murdered?'

'Your family is perfectly well,' laughed Mr Kirwin, 'and you have a visitor. Shall I show him in?'

For some strange reason I thought this was the monster, who had come to laugh at me in my suffering. I put my hand before my eyes and cried out, 'Oh take him away! I do not want to see him. For God's sake, do not let him enter!'

Mr Kirwin frowned. 'Why do you say that?' he said. 'It is only your father.'

'Then show him in! I am sorry. I thought it was someone else.'

Mr Kirwin nodded and left the room. A moment later my father entered.

Back to Switzerland

Nothing, at this moment, could have given me greater pleasure than the arrival of my father. I stretched out my hands to him and cried,

'Are you, then, safe, Papa — and Elizabeth — and Ernest?'

My father calmed me by telling me that everyone was well, and tried to cheer me by talking about the things he knew were so dear to my heart. Then he stared at the chains and the barred windows. 'What a strange place this is, Victor,' he said. 'Unhappiness seems to follow you around. And poor Clerval — '

'Yes,' I gasped. 'I am cursed. I should have died on the coffin of Henry.'

I fainted once again. When I awoke, my father had gone.

Two weeks later, I was freed from prison. The judge found out that I was in the Orkneys at the time of the murder.

I knew that soon I would be back in Geneva, but I was not happy. What did it matter to me whether I lived in a prison or a palace? The cup of my life was poisoned forever. The sun still continued to shine for other people, but I could not see it. I could see nothing but a dense and frightful darkness, and two eyes that stared angrily at me. Sometimes they were the eyes of Henry looking out at me from his coffin. Sometimes they were the watery, clouded eyes of the monster, as I first saw them looking at me in my bedroom in Ingolstadt.

But I decided not to despair. I had a duty to perform. I had to protect my family. I would go back to Geneva and lie in wait for the murderer.

We got on board a ship and sailed away from the shores of Ireland. At midnight I lay on the deck and looked at the stars. I could hear the waves sweeping past the side of the ship below me. I was still ill with the fever. My body had become like a skeleton. I kept thinking of Clerval and the death of my brother. I remembered the mad energy with which I had created the demon. A thousand sad thoughts pressed down upon me and I wept.

I was so depressed, I took a drug given to me by a doctor, which sent me into a deep sleep. But the drug did not stop me from having dreams. Towards morning I had a kind of nightmare. I thought I felt the monster's hands around my neck. I could not break free from him. Groans and cries rang in my ears.

I was awoken by my father. I saw the stars above and heard once more the soft noise of the waves below. The demon was nowhere to be seen. For the time being I was safe. But for how long?

The sea journey came to an end. We landed in France and went to Paris. My father wanted me to meet people. I refused. I was ashamed. I had unchained a monster and set him loose amongst my fellow human beings — a creature who loved more than anything else to spill their blood and laugh with joy at their sufferings and their screams of pain. If they only knew my terrible secret!

My father was getting more and more worried about my behaviour. I told him nothing about the monster, but I kept shouting out that I had killed William, Justine and Henry. This he did not understand, and it upset him greatly.

'I know you are still ill with the fever,' he said, 'but you must not keep saying those things. It is madness. You must promise never to speak like that again.'

'I am not mad,' I cried. 'The sun and the moon have watched me at work. They know I am telling the truth. I am the killer of those innocent victims. They died because of me. I would have spilled my own blood, drop by drop, if I could have saved their lives. But I had to think of the whole human race. I could not sacrifice the whole human race!'

My father decided that I was still in a state of shock, and quickly changed the subject.

As time passed by, I became calmer. A few weeks later, I was strong enough to leave Paris. On the way to Switzerland I received the following letter from Elizabeth.

My dearest Victor,

I am delighted to hear that you will soon be back in Geneva. Your father tells me how much you have suffered. I expect you will be looking even more ill than when you left. I have been very miserable without you. I know that you are still weak from your sickness, but there is something I would like us to talk about very seriously. I must write now while I still have the courage.

You know that your parents were very anxious to see us married. We were told this when we were quite young. We have always been very affectionate, but perhaps you only look upon me as a kind of sister. Is there somebody else, Victor? I must know the answer to this question. Do you love another?

When you left for England, I thought perhaps you were running away from the promise you had made to your parents. I love you, and in my dreams you are always with me. However, if you do not wish to marry me, I will understand.

Do not let this letter disturb you. Don't answer tomorrow or the next day. If it causes you pain, do not even mention it when we meet. Your father will send me news of your health. If you are happy and smiling, I will be overjoyed.

Elizabeth

This letter made me think of the demon's threat, 'I will be with you on your wedding night!' This was my death sentence. On that night, the demon would do all he could to destroy me. On that night, he would end his crimes with my death. Well, let it be so. There would be a fierce and deadly struggle. If he won, I would be at peace and his power over me would end. If he lost, I would be a free man. I gave a bitter laugh. I would be as free as a peasant who has seen his family murdered before his eyes and his cottage burned. I would still be guilty of the death of three people. The only advantage I would gain from such a victory would be the love of Elizabeth.

I read Elizabeth's letter again and again. I loved her with all my heart. I would die to make her happy.

I remembered that the monster had promised to be with me on my wedding night. Supposing I did not marry? The monster would still continue to murder and destroy. After all, he had killed Clerval. What had I to lose? Better to get it over with. With these thoughts in mind, I wrote a letter:

My dearest Elizabeth,

You are the only hope of happiness that is left to me. I love you dearly and we will be married as soon as possible. But I have a secret, Elizabeth. It is a dreadful secret. When I tell you about it, your body will go cold with horror. You will not be surprised that I have been so unhappy. I will tell you this secret the day after our marriage. Until then, you must not say a single word on this subject to me or anybody else.

Your future husband,

Victor.

One week later my father and I returned to Geneva. Elizabeth welcomed me with warm affection, but there were tears in her eyes as well. She saw that my body had almost turned into a skeleton and my cheeks were filled with fever.

To my horror, I began to have fits of uncontrollable anger. 5 Sometimes I would blaze with fury and shout out in a loud voice. Sometimes I would sit in a corner and speak to nobody for hours. It was only the kindness of Elizabeth that stopped me from going completely mad.

The date fixed for our wedding drew nearer. My heart 10 began to sink inside me but I pretended to be happy and cheerful. I began to arm myself in case the demon should make his attack. I carried pistols wherever I went, and this made me feel safer.

During the wedding, Elizabeth became very sad, as if 15 somehow she knew that evil was waiting close by. Perhaps she was worried about my secret.

After the ceremony, we hired a boat and sailed across the lake. Those were the last moments of my life in which I enjoyed the feeling of happiness. The boat moved along 20 quickly. The sun was hot, but we were sheltered by the sail. The scenery was truly beautiful. There were snow-covered mountains and lovely green trees by the shore. Small birds sang as they flew overhead.

I took Elizabeth's hand. 'Why are you so sad?' I asked. 25 'We will not live forever. We should be happy while we can.'

'Don't worry about me,' she replied. 'Deep down I am very happy. But there is a voice that keeps whispering to me. I will not listen to that voice any longer. Look,' she said, 'see how fast the clouds are passing overhead. I can see the 30 tops of the mountains. Look down there! Can you not see all those fish swimming in the clear waters? I can see every stone that lies at the bottom!'

Elizabeth tried to look cheerful, but in her eyes I saw the shadows of fear. I too was afraid. 35

The sun sank lower in the heavens. We passed from the lake into a river and sailed towards a small village. We saw the tower of a church beneath the wooded slopes of hills.

As we approached the shore, the soft wind blew the delightful scent of flowers and hay towards us. The sun sank beneath the horizon, and once again my heart began to freeze with fear.

The monster keeps his promise

It was eight o'clock when we landed. We walked for a short time on the shore. Then we went into the garden of a nearby inn, where we had planned to spend the night. We spent a long time looking at the beauty of the waters, woods and mountains.

But the wind began to rise. It became more and more violent. Clouds swept across the moon. Suddenly a heavy storm of rain fell down from the heavens, and we had to go inside.

I had been calm during the day. But when night came, a thousand fears entered my mind. I was anxious and watchful. I kept hold of the pistol hidden beneath my jacket. Every sound terrified me. I was ready to fight for my life. I had made up my mind that I would not stop fighting until my enemy had been killed.

Elizabeth watched me. She remained silent at first, but then she began to tremble. 'What's the matter, Victor?' she asked. 'What are you so frightened of?'

'Please don't ask questions, my love,' I replied. 'If I live through this night, all will be safe. But this night is dreadful, very dreadful.'

An hour passed by. The demon could strike at any moment. I did not want Elizabeth to get hurt in the fighting, so I told her to go to bed. Then I walked through the passages of the inn looking for the monster. I could not find him anywhere. I began to hope that something might have happened to the creature.

It was then that I heard a shrill and dreadful scream. It came from the room in which Elizabeth had gone to bed. As soon as I heard it, I realized the truth. I must have been blind! The demon had tricked me. My arms dropped in horror. Every muscle in my body seemed to freeze. This state lasted only a fraction of a second. Then I heard a second scream, and I rushed up to the room.

Great God! The sight of it almost killed me. There was Elizabeth, thrown across the bed like a broken doll. Her body was pale and lifeless. Her head hung downwards. The face was twisted out of shape with pain and her dead eyes stared upwards at the ceiling. My head seemed to explode with the shock, and I fell to the ground.

When I recovered, I found myself surrounded by the people of the inn. Their faces were breathless with horror. I pulled myself to my feet and ran to the room where they had taken the corpse of Elizabeth. She had been placed on a table. A handkerchief had been thrown across her face and neck. It seemed as though she were sleeping. I rushed over to her and kissed her. But she was cold. The woman I loved was no more. The marks of the murderer's fingers were on her neck, and no breath came from her lips.

While I still clung to her body in an agony of despair, I happened to look up. I saw a pale, yellow moon shining through the window. The shutters had been thrown back. At the open window stood the huge, terrifying shape of the monster. A twisted grin was on his face. He seemed to be laughing. He pointed with his hellish finger at the corpse of my wife. I rushed to the window and took the pistol from my jacket and fired it at him. But he escaped. He ran with the speed of lightning and plunged into the lake.

The sound of the pistol brought many more people to the room. I pointed to the spot where the monster had been. We went out to search for him, but saw no sign of him anywhere. Several hours later, we returned.

When we got back, I felt very ill. I fell down in a state of utter exhaustion. A mist covered my eyes and my skin was burned dry with the heat of fever. In this state I was carried to my room and placed on the bed. My eyes kept wandering around the room as if looking for something that I had lost.

Some time later, I got up and went back to the room where the body of Elizabeth lay. There were women weeping

around her. I could not think what to do. I
just stared at the body and remembered poor
William, Justine and Clerval. I shuddered. At this
very moment, my father, too, might be twisting around
5 in the grasp of the demon! Was he also to be taken from
me? Was I to be left with nothing? I decided to return to
Geneva with all possible speed.

THE LONG CHASE

The demon escapes

I found that I could not get back to Geneva as quickly as I had hoped. There were no horses for hire, so I had to return across the lake by boat. The wind was fierce and the rain was falling very heavily. However, morning had only just come, so I could expect to reach my home by nightfall quite easily.

I hired some men to row, and took one of the oars myself. Bodily exercise, I thought, would calm me. But after a short while my sorrow was too much, and I could do nothing. I threw down my oar, and held my head in my hands, allowing every gloomy idea that arose to fill my mind. If I looked up, I saw scenes that reminded me of happier times. I had enjoyed them only the day before in the company of my dearest Elizabeth, who was now nothing but a shadow, and a memory. Tears streamed from my eyes. The rain stopped for a moment, and I saw the fish swimming about in the waters. Just a few hours before, Elizabeth had been watching them, too.

There is nothing so painful to the human mind as a great and sudden loss. Whatever happened that day, whether the sun was shining or the rain pouring down, nothing looked to me the same as it had done the day before. A monster had snatched away from me every hope of future happiness. No one had ever been so miserable as me, especially as I had made the creature which was now destroying my own happiness. Truly, such a dreadful thing had never happened to anyone else in the whole of human history.

When I arrived at Geneva, I found that my father and Ernest had not been harmed. However, my father had heard the bad news, and he was seriously ill. I can see him now, that excellent, well-loved old man. His eyes looked about,

this way and that, without paying much attention to anything, for he had lost the one thing that charmed and delighted him most — his Elizabeth. She had been more than a daughter to him. He had loved her with all the affection that
5 a man feels who, in his final years, has few dear friends, and clings more earnestly to those that remain.

Cursed, cursed be the devilish monster that brought unhappiness on his old grey hairs, and doomed him to waste away in wretchedness! Horrors were growing all around him,
10 worse and worse, and his will to live suddenly gave way. Soon he was unable to get out of bed, and a few days later, he died in my arms.

I do not exactly remember what happened to me after that. I lost all sense of where I was. I remember chains, and
15 darkness pressing down on me. Sometimes I dreamt I was walking with the friends of my youth in fields covered with flowers. But, when I woke up, I found myself in a dark cell, and then my sorrows returned and overwhelmed me again. Slowly I began to understand where I was. My friends and
20 neighbours had thought that I was mad, and for many months I had been locked away in a cell. When my mind became clearer, I was set free.

My freedom, however, would have been a worthless thing if I had not used it to set right the cause of these evils. I was
25 filled with a terrible and burning rage when I thought of the monster I had made. I wanted to get my hands on him, and to take a great and awful revenge on his cursed head.

The judge

About a month after my release, I went to a judge. I told
30 him that I knew who the destroyer of my family was, and that I wanted him to use all his power to arrest the wicked murderer. The judge promised that he would do everything he could to catch the criminal, and I therefore asked him to listen to my story.
35 At first the judge seemed to believe nothing I told him, but as I continued, he became more attentive and interested.

I saw him sometimes shudder with horror; at other times he looked greatly surprised, but nevertheless he seemed to realize that I was telling the truth. I finished by asking him to use all his power to seize and punish the monster. I said it was his duty, as a judge, to do this, and his feelings as a man should make him even more determined to take steps to catch the creature.

However, although he was ready to listen to me, he did not seem willing to do anything. 'The creature of whom you speak appears to be too powerful for anyone to capture,' he said. 'Who can follow an animal which can cross the sea of ice and inhabit places where no man would dare to go? Besides, some months have passed since he committed these crimes. No one knows now where he has gone, or where he may be hiding.'

I left the judge's house and returned home to think of some other plan of action.

I was now driven on by my anger, and nothing else. All I could think about was revenge. I was determined to find the monster and kill him. This gave me strength. It calmed my mind and allowed me to calculate and plan at a time when the only other possibility for me was madness and a slow death.

My first decision was to leave Geneva for ever. My own country, which had been so dear to me when I was happy, now in these sad and difficult days, became hateful to me. I collected together a large sum of money and some jewels. Then I began to search for clues that would tell me where the monster was, or where he had gone.

I wandered for hours about the countryside near Geneva. My task seemed hopeless, and I was in despair. It seemed to me that the monster could be many, many miles away by then. When night fell, I found myself outside a cemetery. It was the one where William, Elizabeth and my father had been buried. I entered it and stared at the tomb-stone which marked their graves. Everything was silent except for the leaves of the trees which were being gently shaken by the wind. It was nearly dark and the air felt as if it were filled

with sadness. The ghosts of the dead seemed to fly around.
I could see nothing, but I was sure I could feel their shadows
touching me as they passed.

My misery gave way to anger and frustration. They were
dead, but I was still living. Their murderer, too, was alive
and had not yet been punished. I knelt on the grass and
kissed the earth. My lips trembled and I spoke out loud. 'By
the sacred earth on which I kneel, and by the ghosts all
around, I swear that I will find this murdering demon and
destroy him. While there is still a drop of life left in my body,
I will hunt him down. Let this monster be cursed. Let him
feel the misery he has caused!'

Suddenly, through the stillness of the night, came a loud
and hellish laugh. It rang in my ears, and my blood ran cold.
The laughter died away and then I heard a loud whisper
close to my ear. 'I am satisfied. Miserable wretch! You
have decided to
live, and I am
satisfied.'

I rushed to the spot where the sound had come from, but the devil ran off too quickly for me to catch him. Suddenly the wide circle of the moon rose. It shone upon his ghost-like shape as he ran away from the cemetery with a speed that no living creature could match.   5

The laughing devil

I followed him, and for many months this has been my task. Following small, unimportant clues, I journeyed down the river Rhone from Geneva to the Mediterranean Sea. There, in one of the towns on the coast, I saw the monster boarding   10
a ship which was about to leave for the Black Sea. I managed to get on the same ship, and thought I would at last be able to catch him. But he was well hidden. I looked everywhere for him, but could not find him.

When we reached the end of our journey, I caught sight   15
of him again. I chased him across the wild lands of Tartary and Russia, but he always got away from me. Sometimes terrified peasants told me of a demon they had seen passing through their district, and they showed me where he had gone. Sometimes it seemed that he himself left tracks to guide   20
me. Perhaps he was afraid that if I could not find him, I would give up, and die, and he did not want that to happen. The snows fell and I saw his huge footprints stretching across the white plain. I suffered from cold, hunger and lack of sleep, but these were nothing to me. Inside I was cursed   25
with an endless desire for revenge. I carried my own eternal hell about with me.

And yet it seemed as if, all this time, some good spirit was with me, showing me the way, and, when I cried out with hopelessness, helping me out of the worst difficulties.   30
Sometimes, even in the most deserted of places, when I had dropped to the ground with hunger and tiredness, I would wake to find food placed close by. It was indeed the ordinary sort of food that country people ate in those parts, but it did me good. When I fell down, nearly dead from thirst in hot,   35
dry deserts, with the blue sky bright and clear above me,

it often seemed that some slight cloud would cross the sun and a few drops of rain fall to refresh me.

I do not know what the feelings of the demon were. Sometimes he left messages for me on trees or stones. They guided me, and filled me with anger at the same time. 'My reign is not yet over,' was how one message began. It went on, 'You are still alive, and so my power is complete. Follow me. I am heading for the everlasting ice of the north, where you will feel the misery of cold and frost which cannot harm me. Not far from here you will find some food. Eat it and be refreshed. Come, my enemy! One day we shall fight each other to the death, but you will have to live through many hard and miserable hours before that moment comes.'

How that devil seemed to be laughing at me!

Oh, I cannot tell you how much I hope he suffers torture and death. I will never give up my search until one of us dies. And then with what happiness will I join my dear Elizabeth and my friends, who are even now preparing for me the reward that will come at the end of this dreadful journey.

I journeyed further and further towards the north. The snow began to fall heavily and the weather became almost too cold to bear. The peasants shut themselves up in their huts. Only the bravest would go out to hunt wild animals which were themselves forced, by starvation, to leave their hiding places. The rivers were covered with ice, so it was impossible to catch fish.

My enemy seemed to be more and more pleased as my sufferings increased. One of his messages read as follows:

'Prepare yourself! Your hardships have only just begun. Wrap yourself in furs and provide yourself with food. We shall soon begin a journey where your sufferings will be so great that even my everlasting hatred will be satisfied.'

These words only increased my anger, and my courage and determination. I made up my mind that I would not fail, and I called on heaven to help me.

I continued to cross immense deserts of snow until at last the ocean appeared in the distance. How unlike the blue seas of the south was this! It was completely covered with ice. It was almost impossible to tell where the land ended and the ice began. The Greeks, in the old story, wept for joy when they saw the Mediterranean Sea from the hills of Asia, and knew they were not far from home. I did not weep, but I knelt down and thanked my guiding spirit. It had brought me safely to the place where I hoped I would at last do battle with my enemy.

Some weeks before sighting this frozen ocean, I had bought a sledge and some dogs. With them I was able to cross the snows with unbelievable speed. Gradually, I began to catch up with the monster, and when I first saw the ocean, he was only one day's journey ahead of me. I had hoped to catch him before he reached the shore, and with new courage I hurried on even faster.

I arrived at a tiny collection of huts on the coast. The people who lived there told me that a monster, as large as a giant, had arrived the night before. He had been armed with a gun and many pistols. This creature had frightened away the inhabitants of one of the huts and stolen all their store of winter food. Then he had placed the food on a sledge and taken a team of well-trained dogs. To the joy of the terrified villagers, he had set off across the frozen sea in a direction that led to no land. There, they said, he would be destroyed by the breaking up of the ice, or frozen to death by the everlasting cold.

This information filled me with despair. He had escaped me! I would now have to start on a desperate and almost endless journey across the frozen sea. I would have to face cold so great that few men could live through it, and which was certain to kill me, since I came from a much warmer, sunnier country. But the thought of the demon escaping unpunished for his murders filled me with so much hatred that I paid little attention to anything else. The spirits of the dead seemed to be standing around me, encouraging me to work for their revenge. I must continue this terrible journey and find the monster. I slept for a while, and then I began the chase yet again.

I bought a large supply of food and a new sledge which would travel more easily across the icy hills of the frozen sea. When all was ready, I set off from the land.

On the northern ice

5 I cannot guess how many days have passed since then; but I have endured great misery. Only one thing has made it possible for me to endure such hardship, and that is the desire, ever burning in my heart, to take my revenge on that demon.

10 Often my way was blocked by immense mountains of ice. Many times, when it was not quite so cold, I heard the thunder of the frozen sea beginning to break up. This threatened to destroy me, but then the cold weather returned and made the way safe again.

15 From the amount of food I ate, I guess that I spent three weeks on this journey. Again and again I hoped to set eyes on the monster, and again and again I was disappointed. I came close to giving up completely, and my unhappiness was very nearly too much for me.

20 One evening we reached a huge ice-mountain. The poor animals that pulled my sledge struggled, with immense effort, to the top, and one of them was so exhausted that he died. The thought that yet another innocent creature had been killed because of me filled me with great sorrow. In my 25 wretchedness I sat at the top of this mountain, looking around at the scene before me and not knowing what to do next.

Suddenly my eye caught sight of a dark spot moving across the plain below. I looked harder to see what it could be, and then I shouted out a wild cry of joy when I realized 30 it was a sledge, and on the sledge was an unusually large, but well-known form. Now hope returned, and filled my heart with sudden warmth! Tears filled my eyes. I hastily wiped them away, so that they would not spoil the view I had of the demon. But it was no use. My emotions were so 35 great that I could not control my tears. The burning drops ran down my cheeks, faster and faster, and I wept aloud.

There was no time for delay.
I removed the dog that had died
from the rest of the team, and I gave
the others a good meal and an hour's
rest. This filled me with impatience, but it   5
was absolutely necessary, as they were weak from
their hard climb up the mountain. Then I continued my
journey. The other sledge was still visible; I did not lose sight
of it again except when, from time to time, it was hidden as
it passed behind an ice-rock. Gradually I began to get closer   10
and closer to it, and when, after two days, I saw my enemy
no more than a mile away from me, my heart filled with joy.

But then, when I was almost close enough to catch hold
of him, my hopes were suddenly wiped out. I lost him more
completely than I had ever done before.   15

I heard the sea move beneath the ice. The thunder of the rolling waters became louder and louder. I kept moving on, but it was no use. The wind rose, the sea roared, there was a sudden shudder like that of an earthquake, and the ice split and cracked before my eyes. In a few minutes the sea was rolling between me and my enemy, and I was left drifting on a large piece of ice. Soon it would melt, and I would plunge to a dreadful death in the icy waters.

Many hours passed. Several of my dogs died, and I was almost ready to fall into the sleep of death myself when I saw your ship. I was very surprised, as I had no idea ships sailed so far to the north.

I quickly destroyed part of my sledge and made myself some oars. Then I began to row my ice-raft in the direction of your vessel. I came on board only because you were going northwards in the direction of the demon. If you had been going to the south, I hoped to ask you to let me have a small boat, so that I could continue chasing my enemy.

Oh, when will my guiding spirit lead me to that demon, so that I can destroy him and then go to that rest I desire so much? Or must I die, and leave him alive? If I do, Walton, I would wish to ask you to search for him, and satisfy my revenge by killing him.

But I feel I dare not ask so much of you; to do what I have done, and to suffer the great hardships that I have suffered. I cannot be so selfish. Yet, when I am dead, if you should come across him, if the spirits of revenge should somehow bring him to you, promise me that you will not let him live. Do not allow him to add to the list of his dark crimes.

You must be very careful, for he cannot be trusted. Do not listen to his persuasive words. He is full of cunning and his soul is as hellish as his appearance. When he talks, remember William, Justine, Clerval, Elizabeth, my father, and myself, the wretched Victor Frankenstein. Plunge your sword into his black heart. When you do so, my spirit will be at your side, helping you drive the blade straight in.

THE END OF THE EXPEDITION

Letters written by Robert Walton
to his sister, Margaret

26th August, 17__

Now you know Victor Frankenstein's strange and terrifying story, Margaret. Does it not make your blood freeze 5 *with horror? It affects me greatly when I think about it.*

There were times when Frankenstein himself could hardly continue with his tale. He found it almost too difficult to speak about subjects that were so full of dreadful sorrow for him. At any one moment his eyes would light up with anger, 10 *and then, an instant later, they would fill with tears of the deepest sorrow. Sometimes he was well in control of himself, and would tell me about the most horrible events in a calm, steady voice, his face showing no feeling at all; then, without any warning, his face would suddenly change to an* 15 *expression of the wildest anger and he would shout out the most awful curses on the monster he had created.*

I believe everything he says. The honest, simple way he tells his story suggests it is the truth. Yet I must admit, the letters of Safie and Felix which he had taken from the 20 *monster, and which he showed me, and the sight from our ship of that evil demon driving across the ice on his sledge, convinced me more than anything else.*

Sometimes I have tried to find out how Frankenstein made this creature, but he always refuses to reveal his secret. 'Are 25 *you mad, my friend?' he said once. 'Do you also wish to create a demon that will become a deadly enemy to yourself, and to all those you love? Peace, peace! Learn from my mistakes, and do not try to increase your own.'*

Thus a week has gone by, and I have listened to the strangest tale that anyone could ever imagine. I have spent the whole time thinking about my guest, not only because of the story he tells, but also because of his own noble 5 *character. I wish to soothe him, yet how can I encourage anyone who is so deeply unhappy to continue with his life? I believe that now the only joy he can ever know will be when he composes his broken spirit to peace and death. Yet he enjoys one comfort, which is the result of his being alone* 10 *so much. He believes that, when in dreams he is comforted by seeing and talking to his friends, that these images are not the creations of his own fancy, but in fact the people themselves who come from another world to visit him. He is so convinced about this that when he tells me of his dreams,* 15 *I find them almost as impressive and interesting as the truth.*

We do not only talk about his sad life and misfortunes, but we discuss many other subjects as well. On every point of general literature he is very well informed, and has a quick intelligence. Whenever he speaks, everything he says 20 *is expressed so beautifully. He is very persuasive. I cannot listen to him talking about anything that is sad or emotional, without being moved to tears. What a wonderful person he must have been in happier times: he is so noble and godlike even in ruin! He seems to know his own worth, and to* 25 *understand the greatness of his fall.*

'When I was younger, Walton,' he said to me the other day, 'I believed I would do something great in my life. My feelings were deep and strong, but I also had a clear, calm mind. I knew I was destined for some great achievement. 30 *This feeling of confidence in myself helped me greatly, especially at times when others would have given up. I thought it would be criminal to waste my special abilities on anything less than the most difficult work, when I was so certain that what I did would be of so much value to my* 35 *fellow human beings.*

'When I realized that it would be my task to make a living, thinking, human creature, then I could not regard myself as just an ordinary scientist; but this thought, now,

*only serves to plunge me lower in the dust. All my ideas and
hopes have come to nothing, and like the great angel who
thought he would be God, and who was thrown from
Heaven, I, too, am now chained down in a never-ending
hell. Even now I can clearly remember my thoughts and*   5
*feelings as I worked on the creature. How proud I was of
what I was doing, because I thought I could see that the
result would be so universally good. Even before then my
mind was filled with high hopes, and I imagined that I
would become a very famous person. But look at me now!*   10
Look what I have become!

   *'Oh, my friend, if you had known me as I once was in
earlier, happier days, you would not recognize me now. I
was never sad. I had my friends and my family around me.
My life seemed to be carrying me onwards and upwards*   15
forever, until I fell, never, never again to rise.'

   *Oh, Margaret, my dear sister, how pitiful this is. And must
I now lose this most wonderful being? I have always longed
for a friend. I have been searching so long for someone who
will understand me, sympathize with me and love me, and*   20
*look! Here, in this deserted place, where I expected to find
only loneliness, I have found him. But I fear I have gained
him only to learn of his value, and then lose him. I want
him to live, but he is so full of sorrow he can think only of
his own death.*   25

   *When I spoke to him of my need for his friendship, he
thanked me, but said he believed nothing would ever replace
the friendship of those he had lost — especially Elizabeth
and his boyhood friend, Henry Clerval. 'Wherever I am,' he
said, 'the soothing voice of Elizabeth and the conversation*   30
*of Clerval will be for ever whispered in my ear. They are
both dead now, and there is only one thing that will
persuade me not to join them. If I were doing something
that would be of the greatest usefulness to my fellow-
creatures, then I would want to live until the task were*   35
*finished. But that is not my destiny. All I have left is to chase
after the dreadful creature I made, and destroy him. Then
my work will be done, and I may die.'*

2nd September

My beloved sister,

We are surrounded by great danger, and I do not know if I shall ever see dear England again, or the dearer friends that live there. In the sea all around us are mountains of ice. There is no way past them, and each moment they threaten to crush the ship. The crew are frightened. They look to me to tell them what to do, but I can offer no help.

Frankenstein tries to comfort me and fill me with hope. He reminds me how often the same things have happened to other explorers who have tried to sail across this sea. Even the sailors are persuaded by his words. When he speaks to them, they no longer despair, and he encourages them to work harder. They begin to believe that these enormous masses of ice are nothing that the mind and courage of man cannot deal with. But their feelings of bravery do not last long. Every day that we wait here, surrounded by icebergs and unable to move, their worries increase.

5th September

We are still surrounded and unable to move. The weather is becoming colder and colder. Frankenstein is growing weaker all the time. A fever burns in his eyes and he is easily exhausted by any action.

This morning, as I sat watching the white face of my friend, some sailors came into my cabin. They wanted me to promise to return home if we succeeded in escaping from the mountains of ice.

I was about to reply when Frankenstein sat up and spoke to the men. 'What do you mean? he said. 'You came here looking for glory. You wanted to be explorers. You wanted to be remembered forever by the human race. You knew there would be danger. Are you going to be defeated by your first problem? Do you want to bring shame to your captain and show the world that you are cowards? You must have courage. You must remain as firm as a rock. The ice will

*disappear. It is not as strong as your hearts. Don't return
to your families as failures. Return as heroes who have
fought and conquered and
have never turned their
backs upon the enemy.'*   5

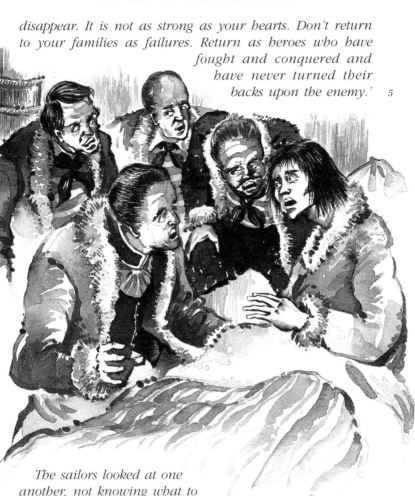

*The sailors looked at one
another, not knowing what to
say. I told them to think again. If
after that they still wanted to go home, I would agree. But
I hoped they would be filled with courage and continue.*   10

*The men left. I looked at my friend. He was now
unconscious. The effort of the speech had been too much for
him.*

*I fear that the men will demand to return home. I am
filled with shame. My dreams of glory are already beginning   15
to fade. It is as though a part of my soul had died.*

7th September

It is all over. The men have reached their decision. I have agreed to return, if we are not destroyed by the icebergs. My hopes have been shattered by their cowardice. I will
5 *return as a failure.*

12th September

The expedition has come to an end. I have given up my dreams of honour and glory. I have lost my friend. I am returning to England. I will write to tell you how it happened
10 *as the wind blows the ship back towards land. Perhaps this will take my mind off the bitter feelings of failure and disappointment which fill my heart.*

On 9th September the ice began to move. Roars like thunder were heard in the distance. Islands of ice split and
15 *cracked in every direction. We were in terrible danger, but we could do nothing but wait. I sat by the side of my friend who was on the point of death. The ice cracked behind us and it was driven towards the north with tremendous force. A breeze came from the west, and on 11th September the*
20 *passage towards the south became perfectly free. When the sailors saw this, they gave a terrific shout of joy. It was loud and continued a long, long time. Frankenstein woke up.*

'Why are they shouting?' he asked.

'They shout because they will soon return to England.'
25 *'Is this true?'*

'Yes,' I replied. 'I can't make them change their minds. I must return with them.'

'You may return,' he said, 'but I will go on. I have a job to do. I dare not fail. I am weak, but the spirits who demand
30 *my revenge will give me strength.' Having said this, he tried to jump out of his bed. But the effort was too great for him. He fell back in a faint.*

It was a long time before he became conscious again. At last he opened his eyes, but he breathed with difficulty and
35 *was unable to speak. The ship's doctor gave him a sleeping*

drug and ordered me not to disturb him. He told me that
my friend did not have many hours left to live.

I sat by Frankenstein's bed and watched him. His eyes
were closed and I thought he was asleep. Then I heard him
speak in a weak voice. He was asking me to come near. He   5
wanted me to hear what he had to say.

'Alas!' he said. 'My strength has gone. I feel that I will
soon die and my enemy will remain alive. I have been
thinking about the past. I created this demon in a fit of
mad enthusiasm and watched him turn against the human   10
race. He became totally evil. He destroyed my friends. He
hates all those happier than himself. I do not know when
his thirst for revenge will end. It was my duty to destroy
him, but I have failed. He still lives, and this worries me.
Otherwise, I would be happy to die. That would be the first   15
real happiness I have known for years.

'I can see the forms of my dead friends moving in front
of my eyes. They fly like angels, and I must hurry to their
arms. Farewell, Walton! Enjoy a peaceful life, and put away
your ambitions. Scientific discoveries can be very dangerous.   20
Yet why should I say this? It is true that my own hopes have
been destroyed, but perhaps another man may succeed.'

His voice became fainter as he spoke. At length he became
exhausted and sank into silence. Half an hour later he tried
to speak again, but he was not able to. I saw his eyes close   25
forever, and a gentle smile disappeared slowly from his lips.

What else is there to say, Margaret? I have lost a friend,
and I return home full of disappointment. Perhaps, however,
I will find some kind of happiness in England.

I am interrupted. What are these sounds that I hear? It   30
is midnight. The breeze is blowing and the watchmen on
deck are silent. Again I hear it! It comes from the cabin
where the dead body of Victor Frankenstein still lies. I must
go and see what is happening. Good night, my sister.

Great God! What a scene has just taken place! The   35
memory of it still makes me dizzy. I have hardly the strength
left to tell you about it.

I entered the cabin where my friend's body had been placed in a coffin. Standing over him was a shape so horrible I can hardly describe it! It was a giant with a terribly deformed, twisted body. As he hung over the coffin,

5 *his face was hidden by his long, ragged hair. He held out one huge hand towards Frankenstein, almost as if he could not believe the man was dead, and appeared to be crying out in grief and horror. He was clearly very shocked. When he heard me come in, he stopped crying and turned quickly*

10 *towards the window, as if to leave. Never had I seen such terrifying ugliness. I shut my eyes in disgust, but called on him to stay.*

He stopped, looking at me with some surprise. Then

15 *he turned again towards the dead man. His huge body shook with the wildest passion.*

'I hunted him just as he hunted me!' he said. 'I thought if I killed the man who had made me this way, my own crimes would be cleared. That became the purpose of my life. But oh, Frankenstein! You god-like, generous being! What use is it now to ask you to pardon me? I destroyed   5
you by destroying all you loved best in this world, but now it is too late to beg your forgiveness. You are cold and cannot answer me!'

His voice choked with emotion. I was curious and felt rather sorry for him. I came nearer but I did not lift my   10
eyes to look at his awful face. I could not bear to look at him. I tried to speak, but the words died away on my lips. The monster continued to groan sorrowfully and blame himself for what had happened. At length I gained enough courage to talk to him.   15

'It is too late to be sorry,' I said. 'If you had been less determined to take your revenge, Frankenstein would still be alive.'

'Do you think, then, that I acted without any feeling of pain or guilt?' he replied. 'Oh, no! Frankenstein did not   20
suffer one ten-thousandth of the pain that was mine. I was torn between my desire for revenge and my guilty conscience. I hated myself for those murders. Frankenstein made my heart so that it would be sensitive to feelings of love and sympathy. When misery forced me into ways of   25
hatred and wickedness, my heart could not endure such a change without hurting me far more than you can ever imagine.'

I was at first touched by the expressions of his misery, yet when I looked at the lifeless form of my friend, my anger   30
returned. 'Your sorrow is caused by your own actions,' I said. 'You are like someone who sets fire to a building, and then sits amongst the ruins crying about what has happened. If Frankenstein were still alive, you would carry on torturing him and making his life a misery. You would still want your   35
revenge. It is not pity you feel. You are only sorry because your victim has at last escaped from your power to hurt him.'

The monster interrupted me. 'That is not true!' he cried. 'Yet I can understand that you should think so. But I am not asking you for any sympathy. I know now that no one will show me any kindness in my life. I am content to suffer alone. Once my mind was filled with hope and goodness. I hoped to meet people who, pardoning my outward form, would love me for the love and goodness which I know is inside me. But now, because of my crimes, I am treated worse than an animal. The fallen angel has become an evil devil.

'Frankenstein has told you of his own sufferings, but he has not told you of mine. All the time I desired love and affection, and I received none. I have sinned against mankind, but mankind has sinned against me. If you hate me, why do you not hate Frankenstein and the others for what they did to me?

'But it is true that I have become evil. I have murdered the lovely and the helpless. I have strangled the weak and innocent as they slept. I have killed those who never did me any harm. And I have caused the death of my creator. There he lies, white and cold in his coffin. You hate me, but you can never hate me as much as I hate myself.

'Do not fear that I shall do any more evil. My work is almost done. I shall leave your ship and go back to the ice-raft that brought me here. Then I will go to the most northern part of the earth and there burn myself to ashes on my own funeral fire. I shall no longer feel all the agonies and frustrations of my wretched life. I shall no longer see the sun or stars or feel the winds play on my cheeks. Death is the only happiness I will ever know.

'Farewell! You are the last person who will ever see me alive. I will rejoice in the agony of the flames. Then the fire will die down, my ashes will be swept into the sea by the winds, and my spirit will sleep in peace. Farewell!'

As he said these words, he jumped from the cabin window onto the ice-raft which lay close to the ship. He was carried away by the waves, and I soon lost sight of him in the darkness and distance.

QUESTIONS AND ACTIVITIES

CHAPTER 1

Use these words to fill the gaps: **knowledge, dreams, anxious, grief, madness, forces, sympathy.**

The stranger was very silent. He often seemed (1) _____, as if he expected to hear bad news. His deep (2) _____ filled Walton with (3) _____. When Walton told him he thought one man's life was a small price to pay for (4) _____ that gave humans power over the (5) _____ of nature, the stranger became very sad. He said such ideas were (6) _____, and when Walton heard what had happened to him, he would give up his (7) _____ for ever.

CHAPTER 2

Put the letters of these words in the right order.

At Ingolstadt Mr Waldman, the (1) **stymerich** teacher, told him how (2) **sintisects** had become the masters of the (3) **endrom** world. Frankenstein decided to become an (4) **proxreel** in the new world of science. He tried to (5) **voscride** what caused living things to become alive. He (6) **indexetremep** on human bodies that he dug up from (7) **varsedgary**. Then one day he (8) **nodursoted** what had until then been a great (9) **symetry** — the secret of life itself.

CHAPTER 3

Put the beginnings of these sentences with the right endings.

1 The monster was by my bed,	(a) in the courtyard.
2 His jaws opened, and he	(b) looking at me.
3 He stretched out his arm	(c) rushed downstairs.
4 I got away and	(d) as if to catch me.
5 I spent the rest of the night	(e) for hours.
6 I walked up and down it	(f) uttered strange sounds.

CHAPTER 4

Find the seven errors in this paragraph.

The day before the murder, Justine had been with her aunt. On her way home someone had told her that William was dead. For several hours she had cried for him. Then, when she tried to get into her house, she found that the gates were unlocked. She spent the night in an inn. Later, the locket that William had worn around his neck fell from Justine's purse. Justine said she could not understand why William might have put it there. She did not know why anyone would want to help her. Justine confessed to the crime. She told Elizabeth that she knew it was the truth. She had only confessed because she had been frightened and the judge had tormented her.

CHAPTER 5

Put the details with the right places.

Place	Details
1 In the shepherd's hut in the forest.	(a) A woman fainted. (b) He ate the old man's breakfast. (c) It was about four feet high. (d) Children began to scream
2 In the house in the village.	(e) He put straw on the floor. (f) He liked the bread, cheese and milk. (g) He blocked the doorway. (h) People threw stones at him.
3 In the small hut in the garden.	(i) There was an old man. (j) There were holes in the walls. (k) He did not like the wine. (l) People ran away in terror.

CHAPTER 6

This is a summary of the conversation between the monster and the old man. Put the old man's replies in the right places.

The Monster	The old man
1 I wish to meet some people here. I love them dearly, and I hope they will love me.	(a) But if you have done nothing wrong, make them believe in your goodness.
2 I am full of fear. If I fail to win their friendship, I will be alone for the rest of my life.	(b) I wish you good luck.
3 I fear that they will be prejudiced against me. They will think of me as a monster.	(c) Tell me your story; perhaps I can make them believe in your goodness.
4 I hope to do that, but they will think I will hurt them. I must overcome this prejudice	(d) Do not despair. The hearts of men are full of love. Be hopeful.

CHAPTER 7

Choose the right words.

The monster said if he had a companion, he would be at peace with (1) **himself / mankind**. But if he remained alone, he would make the world as (2) **mysterious / miserable** as he was. Frankenstein thought if the monster had a companion, he might become (3) **good / worse**; if not, he would become a murdering (4) **machine / madman**. He could attack towns and (5) **valleys / villages**. Frankenstein agreed to help the monster on one (6) **condition / rule**. He made him (7) **believe / swear** that he would leave every place (8) **undeveloped/inhabited** by man. If he agreed to do this, Frankenstein would give him a female.

CHAPTER 8

Why didn't Frankenstein want to make the female monster? Put the words at the ends of these sentences in the right order.

1 She might be ten   [than] [mate] [more] [her]
   thousand times   [evil].
2 She had made no promise   [civilized] [to] [the] [leave]
                               [world].
3 The demon might be   [the] [the] [female] [sight] [of].
   disgusted by
4 She might turn   [disgust] [from] [him] [in].
5 They might create more   [conquer] [the] [would] [who]
   devils   [world].

CHAPTER 9

Which are the best answers?

1 'If I survive this night, all will be safe. But this night is dreadful, very dreadful.' Frankenstein's words show that (a) he expected the monster to attack him; (b) he was frightened of the bad weather; (c) he thought Elizabeth was in danger.
2 When he was walking through the passages of the inn, Frankenstein began to think something had happened to the monster because (a) he thought the storm might have injured him; (b) he could not find him; (c) he had shot the monster.
3 'As soon as I had heard this sound, I realized the truth.' The truth was that (a) the monster's threat was against Elizabeth; (b) the monster was too afraid to attack his own creator; (c) there was nothing to worry about.
4 The monster appeared at the window with a twisted grin on his face. He was pleased (a) to have killed Elizabeth; (b) to have escaped without getting shot; (c) to have caused Frankenstein so much unhappiness.

CHAPTER 10

Put these sentences in the right order. The first one is correct.

1 I chased the monster all across Tartary and Russia.
2 Then the ice cracked, and I could not follow him.
3 I saw his footprints crossing the white plains.
4 I reached a huge ice-mountain and sat on top of it.
5 Many hours later I saw your ship.
6 Two days later, he was no more than a mile away.
7 I bought a sledge for travelling over the frozen sea.
8 I went further north, across deserts of snow.
9 I set off from the land.
10 I reached some huts on the coast.
11 I caught sight of a sledge, with the monster on it.

CHAPTER 11

Which of these did the monster say when he spoke to Walton?

1 'It is true that I have become evil. I have murdered the lovely and the helpless.'
2 'If Frankenstein were still alive, I would carry on torturing him and making his life a misery.'
3 'Frankenstein did not suffer one ten-thousandth of the pain that was mine.'
4 'I am only sorry because my victim has at last escaped from my power to hurt him.'

Oxford
Progressive
English Readers

GRADE 1

Alice's Adventures in Wonderland
Lewis Carroll

The Call of the Wild and Other Stories
Jack London

Emma
Jane Austen

The Golden Goose and Other Stories
Retold by David Foulds

Jane Eyre
Charlotte Brontë

Little Women
Louisa M. Alcott

The Lost Umbrella of Kim Chu
Eleanor Estes

Tales From the Arabian Nights
Edited by David Foulds

Treasure Island
Robert Louis Stevenson

GRADE 2

The Adventures of Sherlock Holmes
Sir Arthur Conan Doyle

A Christmas Carol
Charles Dickens

The Dagger and Wings and Other Father Brown Stories
G.K. Chesterton

The Flying Heads and Other Strange Stories
Edited by David Foulds

The Golden Touch and Other Stories
Edited by David Foulds

Gulliver's Travels — A Voyage to Lilliput
Jonathan Swift

The Jungle Book
Rudyard Kipling

Life Without Katy and Other Stories
O. Henry

Lord Jim
Joseph Conrad

A Midsummer Night's Dream and Other Stories from Shakespeare's Plays
Edited by David Foulds

Oliver Twist
Charles Dickens

The Prince and the Pauper
Mark Twain

The Stone Junk and Other Stories
D.H. Howe

Stories from Shakespeare's Comedies
Retold by Katherine Mattock

The Talking Tree and Other Stories
David McRobbie

Through the Looking Glass
Lewis Carroll

GRADE 3

The Adventures of Tom Sawyer
Mark Twain

Around the World in Eighty Days
Jules Verne

The Canterville Ghost and Other Stories
Oscar Wilde

David Copperfield
Charles Dickens

Fog and Other Stories
Bill Lowe

Further Adventures of Sherlock Holmes
Sir Arthur Conan Doyle

Great Expectations
Charles Dickens